Texas Assess...
Preparation

Grade 4

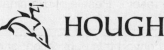

TEXAS
JOURNEYS

TEXAS
WRITE
SOURCE

HOUGHTON MIFFLIN HARCOURT

Contents

How To Use This Book

Texas Assessment Preparation is designed to help you practice for the Texas reading and writing assessments. This book includes sections on Reading, Writing, Revising, and Editing.

- **Reading**   This section includes passages of literature in a variety of literary genres. A **genre** is a type of literature, such as fiction, expository nonfiction, or poetry. Helpful **Tips** guide you as you read the passages and answer the questions about them.

- **Writing**   This section provides prompts for writing one-page personal narratives and one-page expository compositions. Models of student writing show you what to do (and not do) in order to write well.

- **Revising and Editing**   These sections provide practice for improving your writing before creating a final draft.

Get Credit for Your Answers

- **Multiple-Choice Questions**   Your teacher will give you an Answer Document before you begin your work. Fill in each correct answer bubble completely. Check your work. Be sure you have not skipped an item or filled in more than one bubble for an item.

- **Writing Prompts**   You may use a separate sheet of paper to write a first draft for each writing prompt. Always write as clearly as possible. Be sure that your final draft is no more than one page long.

Read the Signs

As you work through this book, you will see the signs and symbols below. Be sure you understand what they mean and what to do when you see them.

Read this selection.	Words in a box give directions. Read them carefully to make sure you understand what to do.
In paragraph 10, the word <u>genre</u> means —	Pay attention to underlined words in a passage. These words will appear later in questions about the passage.
What is the **BEST** way to revise sentence 7?	Boldfaced, capitalized words in test items help you eliminate weaker answer choices.
GO ON ▶	This symbol tells you to go on to the next page.
(STOP)	This symbol means that you should put your pencil down.

5

Texas Assessment
Practice

Fiction

Genre Overview

Fiction refers to a story that is made up. **Realistic fiction** is a made-up story that could take place in real life. A **fantasy** is a made-up story that could not take place in real life.

In every fiction story, there is at least one **character**, at least one **setting**, and a **plot**. These elements are organized into a **story structure**. The author puts them together in a way that will best tell the story.

As you read a fiction story, identify the **characters**. Ask yourself, *Who is this story mostly about?* That person is the **main character**.

The **setting** is the time and place in which the story happens. To identify the setting, ask yourself, *Where and when does this story take place?*

The **plot** is what happens in a story. The plot is made up of a series of events. The **conflict**, or **problem**, is introduced at the beginning of the story. The **resolution**, or **solution** to the problem, is how the problem is solved.

Often, you will be required to **make inferences** about the elements of the story structure, which involves using clues in the text and prior knowledge. Making inferences might also include comparing and contrasting story elements, such as characters and events, across similar texts. For example, you might be asked to compare two similar folktales or fairy tales.

In a story, the **narrator** is the person who tells, or narrates, a story. When planning a work of fiction, the author must decide who that narrator will be.

When a character tells the story, he or she is called a **first-person** narrator. A first-person narrator uses words like *I* and *we* to tell the story.

When the narrator is not a character in the story, he or she is called a **third-person** narrator. A third-person narrator tells the story using words such as *he, she,* and *they.*

Name _____ Date _____

Fiction

Read this selection. Then answer the questions that follow it. Fill in the circle of the correct answer on your answer document.

Two Cinderellas

Yeh-Shen

adapted from a Chinese folktale

1   Once upon a time there was a beautiful girl named Yeh-Shen who lived with her stepmother and stepsister. They were jealous of Yeh-Shen's beauty and kindness, so they were cruel to her. Yeh-Shen was very sad and lonely. Her only friend was a goldfish with big, glowing eyes.

2   The stepmother made Yeh-Shen work very hard. Yeh-Shen never had enough to eat, but she shared the little food she had with her beloved fish.

3   One night the stepmother caught Yeh-Shen feeding the goldfish. "Why are you wasting food on that creature?" asked the stepmother. "You will never see it again!" With that, the stepmother snatched the fish away.

4   Yeh-Shen lay in her bed, crying for her friend. Suddenly, an old man appeared at her door. He said to her, "If you keep the memory of your beloved goldfish in your heart, he will always be there to help you in times of trouble."

5   In the spring, all of the young ladies and gentlemen wanted to attend the Spring Festival. Yeh-Shen wanted desperately to go to the party, but her stepmother refused. "What would you wear, anyway?" she said cruelly before leaving for the festival.

6   Yeh-Shen called out for help to her beloved fish. Suddenly she was wearing a cape of feathers and beautiful golden slippers!

> **Tip**
>
> Think about the words "Yeh-Shen" and "her" in the first paragraph. What do these clues tell you about the narrator of the story?

> **Tip**
>
> Stop every few paragraphs to summarize the main events so far. Think about what might happen next.

9

7   Yeh-Shen went to the Spring Festival and danced with a handsome young man until her stepmother saw her. Yeh-Shen became so frightened that she ran all the way home, losing a slipper on the way.

8   The slipper was brought to the king. He wanted to find the owner, so he asked all the ladies to come and try it on their feet. But no one could wear the slipper—it was too small.

9   One night, Yeh-Shen snuck into the palace to try on the slipper. The king's servants caught her. "Who is this poor girl who wants to try the slipper?" they asked, looking at her tattered clothes. The king was angry with her until he noticed her tiny feet.

10   Yeh-Shen tried on the slipper and it fit. The king asked her to marry him, for he was the young man who had danced with her at the festival. Yeh-Shen accepted the king's proposal, and she lived happily ever after in the palace.

Little Havroshechka

adapted from a Russian folktale

11   Long ago, there lived a poor little girl named Havroshechka. She lived with a cruel mistress and her three daughters, who were all very mean to her.

12   Every day, the mistress told Havroshechka to sew and spin a mountain of clothing, which was terribly hard work. The daughters sat in the sunshine watching Havroshechka as she suffered.

13   One day, Havroshechka told the kind cow in the barn about her troubles. "My poor little girl," said the cow, "I can help with your work. All you have to do is look into my ear, and all your work will be done." She looked into the cow's ear and suddenly all of her work was finished!

Tip

This type of fiction is called "fantasy." What details tell you that this story could not happen in real life?

GO ON

Grade 4: Fiction

14   Havroshechka did this day after day, until the mistress found out about the cow. As the mistress took the cow away, the animal whispered to Havroshechka, "Don't forget me, and I will help you in your time of trouble."

15   Havroshechka did not forget the cow, and she planted an apple tree where the cow had grazed, hoping one day for the cow to be returned. She watered it every day and it grew big and strong.

16   One day, a handsome young man rode his horse by the tree. Seeing the juicy, red apples, he called out, "Dear girls, I will marry the one who brings me a delicious apple from that glorious tree."

17   The mistress's three daughters each tried to grab an apple, but the branches of the tree swung upward, out of their reach. The girls were furious! As little Havroshechka approached, she thought about the cow who had helped her. The tree slowly lowered a branch, and she plucked an apple for the young gentleman. Havroshechka and the young man eventually married and lived happily ever after.

Tip
Think about the conflict, or problem, introduced early in the story. What event solves that problem?

1 How do you know these passages are fiction?

A They give facts and details about real events.

B They tell about real people and their lives.

C They describe events that could not happen in real life.

D They give steps that tell how to do something.

TEKS RC-4(D)

Tip
Think about what makes a passage fiction or nonfiction.

2 Both Yeh-Shen and Havroshechka receive help from—

F godmothers

G animals

H kings

J slippers

TEKS 4.3B

3 Who is telling the Cinderella story from China?

A Yeh-Shen

B The king

C Yeh-Shen's stepmother

D An unknown narrator

TEKS 4.6C

4 Yeh-Shen cries because she—

F misses her friend

G does not have nice clothes

H cannot go to the festival

J has nothing to eat

TEKS 4.6B

Tip
Reread what happens in the story right before Yeh-Shen cries.

GO ON

Grade 4: Fiction

5 Use the chart to answer the question below.

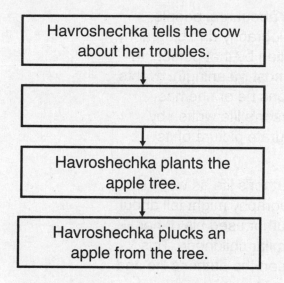

Havroshechka tells the cow about her troubles.

Havroshechka plants the apple tree.

Havroshechka plucks an apple from the tree.

Which of the following belongs in the empty box?

A Havroshechka waters the apple tree.

B A young man rides his horse by the house.

C Havroshechka looks into the cow's ear.

D The young man and Havroshechka are married.

TEKS 4.6A

6 Which sentence best describes the resolution of the conflict in the Cinderella story from Russia?

F Havroshechka must plant an apple tree to find the cow that was taken from her.

G Havroshechka is saved from a terrible life when she gives a man an apple.

H Havroshechka stands up to her cruel stepsisters and eats an apple.

J Havroshechka runs away from home to grow delicious apples.

TEKS RC-4(E)

Tip
Think about Havroshechka's problem, introduced early in the story. What event solves that problem?

Grade 4: Fiction

Literary Nonfiction

Genre Overview

Literary nonfiction is a form of writing that tells about real people, places, or events. Literary nonfiction includes autobiography and biography. An **autobiography** is the story of a person's life written by that person. In writing an autobiography, an author tells about the most meaningful events in his or her life. The author might also include lessons he or she has learned over time. A **biography** is the story of a person's life written by someone else. A good biography creates a full, accurate picture of its subject.

A biography about an author may discuss the author's life as well as details about the author's works. For example, a biography might tell about an author's childhood and then describe how the author used his or her life experiences to write about a character with a similar childhood. This information can help you **make connections** between the author's life and his or her work.

An author might also include other types of **media** that contribute to the overall meaning of the text, such as an advertisement, poster, Web site, or e-mail. These media might show certain words that are bigger than other words on a page, or they might use pictures to catch a reader's attention.

Sometimes an author will tell why important events happened. Other times, you will have to **make inferences**, or use clues in the text to figure out what happened. You may also be asked to **draw conclusions** about what you have read. Always look for **text evidence** to support your conclusions.

Authors use **sensory language** to help readers see, hear, or feel something. Sensory language includes similes and metaphors. **Similes** include the words *like* or *as* to compare two things. An example of a simile is *The tree is as tall as a mountain*. This simile describes a tree that is very tall. **Metaphors** compare two things by saying that one thing *is* another thing. An example of a metaphor is *The girl who led the people was a lion*. This metaphor describes a girl who is strong and brave. Metaphors do not use the words *like* and *as* to compare.

In addition, as you read you might come across words that you do not know. To figure out the meaning of such words, look for clues in the sentence or in surrounding sentences. Often, you can figure out the word's meaning by understanding the **context** in which it is used.

14

Grade 4: Literary Nonfiction

Name _____ Date _____

Literary Nonfiction

Read this selection. Then answer the questions that follow it.
Fill in the circle of the correct answer on your answer document.

Beverly Cleary

1   Beverly Cleary is the author of many children's books
that are bestsellers. She has won awards for stories
about characters such as Ramona Quimby and Henry
Huggins. Yet Beverly struggled to learn to read when
she was young.

2   She was born Beverly Atlee Bunn in 1916, in
McMinville, Oregon. Until she was six years old, she
lived on a small farm. Her mother loved to read stories to
Beverly.

3   When Beverly was six years old, she and her family
moved to Portland, Oregon. It was hard for Beverly to
adjust to a new school. She thought the reading
schoolbooks were very <u>dull</u>. The characters were not
interesting to her. Beverly also became ill and missed
many days of school. When she returned, she struggled
to read at the same level as other students. School
became a dark cloud of confusion for her.

4   When she entered the third grade, Beverly's reading
skills improved. The school librarian helped her find
interesting books to read. She also encouraged Beverly
to write.

5   Beverly graduated from high school and went to
college. One day, she met Clarence Cleary. They later
got married.

> **Tip**
>
> Do you think Beverly liked
> books as a little girl? Why or
> why not?

> **Tip**
>
> Remember that only important
> events should be included in a
> summary. Which events do
> you consider to be important
> up to this point?

Grade 4: Literary Nonfiction

6   Beverly still dreamed of writing stories, but she knew that she also needed a steady job. She worked as a librarian in a small town in the state of Washington. There, she found that some of the children were bored with reading, just as she had been when she was young. "Where are the books about the kids like us?" asked one of the boys.

7   Beverly thought about that boy when she began to write her first book, *Henry Huggins*. The main character of her story was like many of the children she had worked with in the library. His name was Henry, and he was an ordinary third-grade boy. Henry wasn't rich, super-smart, or extremely handsome. He was just an average kid. Henry was also an only child, just as Beverly was.

8   In the story, Henry lives on Klickitat Street. This is a real street only a few blocks from where Beverly used to live in Portland, Oregon. Henry, his dog Ribsy, and his friends were similar to the children Beverly had grown up with.

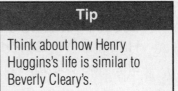

Tip

Think about how Henry Huggins's life is similar to Beverly Cleary's.

9   *Henry Huggins* was published in 1950, when Beverly was 34 years old. The book became a bestseller. Beverly went on to write many other books for children. In all her books, Beverly writes about characters that kids can understand. Beverly's books are still read by children all over the world.

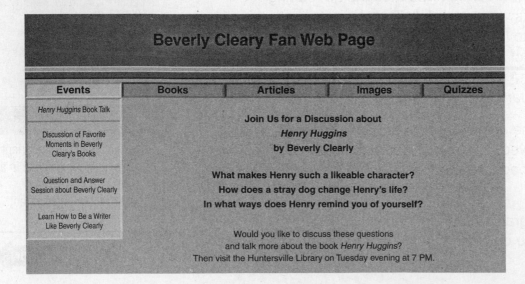

Beverly Cleary Fan Web Page

Events	Books	Articles	Images	Quizzes

Henry Huggins Book Talk

Discussion of Favorite Moments in Beverly Cleary's Books

Question and Answer Session about Beverly Clearly

Learn How to Be a Writer Like Beverly Clearly

Join Us for a Discussion about
Henry Huggins
by Beverly Clearly

What makes Henry such a likeable character?
How does a stray dog change Henry's life?
In what ways does Henry remind you of yourself?

Would you like to discuss these questions
and talk more about the book *Henry Huggins*?
Then visit the Huntersville Library on Tuesday evening at 7 PM.

GO ON

1 What is the meaning of <u>dull</u> as used in paragraph 3?

   A Not bright

   B Not sharp

   C Boring

   D Slow-moving

TEKS 4.2B

Tip
Use clues in the surrounding sentences to help you figure out what *dull* means here.

2 Why does the author compare Beverly's experience to "a dark cloud of confusion" in paragraph 3?

   F To describe how Beverly felt because she was too sick to go to school

   G To describe how angry Beverly was that she had to go to a new school

   H To show that it rained often in Portland when Beverly went to school

   J To show that it was hard for Beverly to clearly understand lessons at school

TEKS 4.8

3 What is the best summary of Beverly's childhood?

   A Beverly experienced some challenges in her childhood and she struggled to read. This changed in the third grade when a librarian helped her with her reading and writing.

   B Beverly did not like to read until her mother read stories to her as a small child. She started writing about interesting characters when she grew up.

   C The librarian at Beverly's school helped to teach Beverly how to read. She told Beverly that she should write a book about herself.

   D School was not easy for Beverly, but she learned to read at the library. She also wrote a book later on when she was older. She wanted to be a librarian.

TEKS RC-4(E)

Tip
Remember that the information in the summary should be only about Beverly's childhood, and it should be supported by the details in the passage.

Grade 4: Literary Nonfiction

Name _____ Date _____

4 Use the chart to answer the question below.

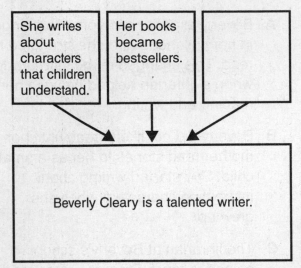

She writes about characters that children understand.

Her books became bestsellers.

Beverly Cleary is a talented writer.

Which of the following details belongs in the empty box?

F She struggled to learn to read.

G She won awards for her stories.

H She is an only child.

J She went to college.

TEKS RC-4(D)

5 How is the character of Henry Huggins similar to Beverly Cleary when she was young?

A Both wanted to be writers.

B Both had a dog named Ribsy.

C Both lived in the same neighborhood.

D Both had to go to a new school.

TEKS 4.7

6 Why does the Web page most likely include questions about the book *Henry Huggins*?

F To show that authors want to learn more about this book

G To get readers to want to come to the book talk

H To suggest that the book is missing information

J To describe why readers should read all of Beverly Cleary's books

TEKS 4.14

Tip
What does the text at the bottom of the Web page ask you?

Grade 4: Literary Nonfiction

Name _____   Date _____

Expository Text

TEKS 4.2E, 4.11A, 4.11D,
4.13B, RC-4(D), RC-4(E)

Genre Overview

Expository text gives facts and information about a topic. All expository text has a **main idea**, or central topic, upon which the text is focused. Additional information about the main idea is given through **supporting details**. Authors write expository text for a certain **purpose**, or reason. They might write to give you information about a topic or to explain how to do something.

While reading expository text, you might find it helpful to periodically summarize what you have learned. **Summarizing** means restating the main ideas in your own words. When you summarize text, only include the important information in the passage. Do not include details that are unimportant or unnecessary.

Expository text includes **text features**, such as guide words, headings, topic sentences, and concluding sentences. **Guide words** at the top of the page and **headings** at the beginning of a section help you find different ideas within the text. **Topic sentences** at the beginning of a paragraph tell you what the paragraph or text will be about. **Concluding sentences** provide summaries of paragraphs or of whole texts to help you understand them.

Expository text might also include **graphic features**, such as charts, diagrams, graphs, and illustrations. Authors use graphic features to present information visually. For example, an author might include a map to show where something took place, or a graph to compare numbers of things.

While reading expository text, you might find it useful to refer to a **dictionary** to help you learn the pronunciation and meaning of new words. Understanding the structure of a dictionary entry can help you quickly locate definitions for unknown words.

Grade 4: Expository Text

Expository Text

Read this selection. Then answer the questions that follow it.
Fill in the circle of the correct answer on your answer document.

The New Science of Sleep

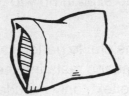

1   Do you feel rested and alert right now? If you do not, then you have a great deal of company. Recent studies suggest that most Americans sleep less than they should. Some people believe that being able to function with less sleep is a sign of willpower. They could not be more wrong. Sleeping is an important part of a healthful life. You should plan your day to give yourself plenty of time to sleep.

A Strong Body

2   Lack of sleep can lead to serious consequences. For one thing, it can damage your health. No one is really sure why the body needs sleep, but people who go with too little sleep for long periods of time can become weak and sick. The body has trouble fighting off disease when it is tired. For reasons that are not yet clear, people who sleep too little also tend to gain weight. One common response to being tired is overeating.

> **Tip**
>
> Note the topic sentence for each paragraph as you read. These sentences will help you remember what each paragraph was about.

A Strong Mind

3   Sleep is not just important for your body, but also for your mind. Your mind needs enough rest every night. Scientists believe that sleeping and dreaming are necessary in order to form lasting memories. In one study, students who learned a new task were tested on it the next day. Those who slept for less than six hours performed as if they were relearning the task from the

> **Tip**
>
> Look for details that support the main idea of each paragraph and the main idea of the passage.

GO ON ➡

beginning. Those who had slept for more than six hours showed that they remembered what they learned. Sleep also affects your mood. People who need sleep often become angry, <u>irritable</u>, or depressed.

Being Safe

4   If you sleep too little, you may also become a danger to those around you. People who drive when they are drowsy are more likely to have accidents. Since sleepiness can lead to poor decision-making, people with jobs that can affect lives, such as doctors or airplane pilots, must be sure to get enough sleep.

Being Smart

5   Of course, once in a while everyone has a sleepless night. Taking a nap or catching up on your sleep the next night will help. However, if you find yourself waking up tired and dragging yourself to school or work day after day, it is time to commit to a better sleep schedule. Go to bed a little earlier every day for several days. Avoid too much activity right before bed. Before you know it, you will face the day fully rested. Getting the proper amount of sleep is not laziness. It is the smart, responsible thing to do.

> **Tip**
>
> If you are unsure of the meaning of words like *commit* or *activity*, use a dictionary to help you understand them.

How Much Sleep Do You Need?

Age	Hours of Sleep Needed
Infants	14–15 hours
Toddlers	12–14 hours
Preschoolers	11–13 hours
School-age Children	10–11 hours
Teenagers	9–10 hours
Adults	8–9 hours

Grade 4: Expository Text

Name _____ Date _____

1 Use the chart to answer the question below.

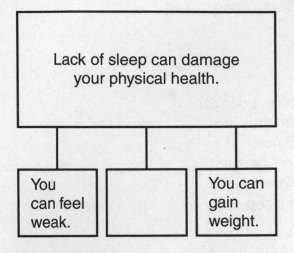

Lack of sleep can damage your physical health.

| You can feel weak. | | You can gain weight. |

Which of the following details best fits in the empty box?

A You can make poor decisions.

B It is harder to fight off disease.

C You can be in a bad mood.

D It is difficult to remember things.

TEKS 4.11A

Tip
The top box contains a main idea. Look for details that support the main idea.

2 Based on its topic sentence, what is paragraph 3 most likely about?

F How lack of sleep affects your mind

G How you can use your mind to fall asleep

H How your mind can help you feel less tired

J How the act of sleeping is all in your mind

TEKS 4.11D

3 Read this dictionary entry for the word irritable in paragraph 3.

irritable \ˈir-ə-tə-bəl\ *adjective* easily annoyed or angered

Based on the dictionary entry, how many syllables are in the word irritable?

A One

B Two

C Three

D Four

TEKS 4.2E

Tip
Syllables are separated by hyphens in a dictionary entry.

GO ON

Grade 4: Expository Text

4 Which sentence from the passage supports the idea that lack of sleep can be dangerous to others?

F *Some people believe that being able to function with less sleep is a sign of will power.*

G *Those who slept for less than six hours performed as if they were relearning the task from the beginning.*

H *People who drive when they are drowsy are more likely to have accidents.*

J *However, if you find yourself waking up tired and dragging yourself to school or work day after day, it is time to commit to a better sleep schedule.*

TEKS RC-4(D)

5 According to the chart, which of the following is true?

A You need the most sleep when you are a teenager.

B You need the same amount of sleep at any age.

C You need more sleep as you get older.

D You need less sleep as you get older.

TEKS 4.13B

Tip
Check the hours of sleep needed at each age. What pattern do you notice?

6 What is the best summary of the passage?

F Americans sleep less than they should. People should plan their day with time for enough sleep. You can become weak or sick if you do not get enough sleep. You can also gain weight from overeating.

G Sleeping is an important part of a healthful life. If you do not get enough sleep, your body and your mind suffer. You can also be a danger to others. There are things you can do to make sure you get enough sleep.

H Most people do not get enough sleep, but it is important to do so. You can go to bed earlier. Do not do anything active, such as exercising, before going to bed or you will have trouble falling asleep.

J Sleep is the most important part of your day. Getting enough sleep helps you feel better and gets you in a good mood. People like doctors need to get a lot of sleep in order to do their jobs well.

TEKS RC-4(E)

Drama

Genre Overview

A **drama**, or play, tells a story through the words and actions of characters. A drama may be performed in a theater or on a school stage, or it may simply be read aloud.

A longer drama may be divided into sections called **acts**. Acts may then be divided into smaller sections called **scenes**. The setting may change in each scene.

A drama has a **cast of characters**. A character's name, followed by a colon, tells who is speaking. For example:

MRS. LEE: Hi, Angela! How did you like the game?

There is very little description in a drama. Almost all of the information is given through speech. The **stage directions** in a drama provide information such as the time and place of the story or a description of the setting. For example:

> *(Time: Present. Setting: The main office of an elementary school in Houston, Texas.)*

Stage directions may describe a character's feelings and actions. For example:

> **MRS. LEE:** *(Smiling)* I think this was our best season ever.
> **MR. DAVIS:** I agree. *(He places the trophy in the case.)*

Stage directions are given from the point of view of an actor on the stage. For example, *stage right* means to the actor's right, which is to the audience's left.

When planning a drama, as in planning any story, the author must decide how one event will follow another. This order, or **sequence**, of events leads the reader or audience through the action of a play to its conclusion.

Name _____ Date _____

Drama

> **Read this selection. Then answer the questions that follow it.**
> **Fill in the circle of the correct answer on your answer document.**

Lost and Found

> **Cast of Characters:** MRS. LOPEZ, JOHN,
> ANDREW, GIRL, FATHER

Scene 1 (*Setting: A street in the present time.*
JOHN and ANDREW enter stage right, chatting.)

1   **JOHN:** Did you see our kickball game at recess?
(*He stops walking and holds up his hand, listening.*)
Hey, do you hear something?

2   **ANDREW:** Yeah, it sounded like it was over here.
(*He walks to a bush, reaches behind it, and picks up a
kitten with a bell on its collar.*) What are you doing back
there, little guy?

3   **JOHN:** Hey, Andrew, do you think we can keep him?
Dad said we could get a cat soon.

4   **ANDREW:** I don't know. Let's go home and ask.

(*Both walk offstage.*)

Scene 2 (*Setting: The BOYS' house. They are sitting on
the floor petting the kitten. MRS. LOPEZ walks in.*)

5   **MRS. LOPEZ:** Where did that kitten come from?

6   **ANDREW:** We found him by a bush down the street.

7   **JOHN:** (*Jumps up and runs over to his mother,
eager.*) Can we keep him? Can we keep him?

8   **MRS. LOPEZ:** (*Looking thoughtful.*) He has a collar
on, so someone has been taking care of him. He
probably ran outside and got lost. The owner must be
looking for him.

9   **JOHN:** Oh. (*Looks disappointed, then perks up.*)
But what if no one is? Then can we keep him?

> **Tip**
>
> In this scene, what happens
> that is unusual? This event
> introduces the problem in
> the play.

> **Tip**
>
> Notice that the stage directions
> are set in italic type. The
> characters do not read
> them aloud.

GO ON

Grade 4: Drama

10   **MRS. LOPEZ:** Well, let's try to find the owner first. Why don't you make posters to put up in the neighborhood? If no one claims the kitten, then maybe we'll keep him.

11   **ANDREW:** I'll get some paper and markers!

(The stage lights go down.)

Scene 3 *(Setting: The street. JOHN is holding the kitten. ANDREW is taping a poster to a pole. A TEENAGE GIRL and her FATHER enter stage right, looking from side to side.)*

Tip

As you read the play, think about how one event leads to another.

12   **GIRL:** Simon! Here, kitty, kitty, kitty! Aw, Dad, we'll never find him! I should have held him while I was doing my homework.

13   **FATHER:** Let's keep looking. He's probably nearby.

(JOHN watches them approach. He starts to speak.)

14   **JOHN:** Um. Are you looking for an orange kitten?

15   **GIRL:** *(Excited)* Yes! That's my kitten! That's Simon!

16   **ANDREW:** We found him when we were walking home. *(JOHN looks sad.)* Come on, John. Hand him over.

17   **JOHN:** *(To ANDREW, in a low voice)* Now I'll never see him again!

(JOHN hands the kitten to the GIRL.)

18   **GIRL:** Thank you so much. *(She studies JOHN's face.)* Hey! We live right over there. You can still visit him!

19   **JOHN:** Really? I can?

20   **GIRL:** Sure. You guys can play with him while I do my homework. Then he won't run off again.

21   **JOHN:** Great! That's what we'll do!

(All walk offstage.)

Tip

Look for an event that resolves the problem introduced at the beginning.

GO ON ➡

1 How can you tell that this is a drama?

   A It is told through words and actions.

   B It has a cast of characters.

   C It has stage directions.

   D All of the above

TEKS 4.5

2 Use the web to answer the question.

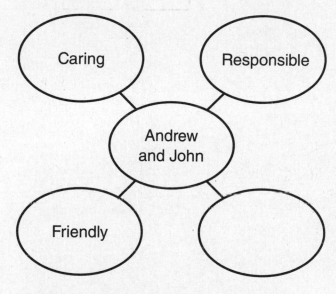

Which of these belongs in the circle?

   F Confused

   G Grateful

   H Greedy

   J Kind

TEKS 4.6B

> **Tip**
> Think about the things that Andrew and John do at the beginning, middle, and end of the play.

3 Which of the following is **NOT** a stage direction?

   A *(Setting: The street.)*

   B *(JOHN looks sad.)*

   C **JOHN:** Really? I can?

   D *(All walk offstage.)*

TEKS 4.5

> **Tip**
> Which answer choice does not describe either a setting or a character's feelings or actions?

4 The stage direction *Turn stage left* means an actor should turn —

   F to his or her left

   G to his or her right

   H to the audience's left

   J in a circle

TEKS 4.5

GO ON

Grade 4: Drama

Name _____   Date _____

5 What event introduces the problem?

A John and Andrew go to school.

B John talks about kickball.

C Andrew finds a kitten.

D John and Andrew take the kitten home.

TEKS 4.6A

Tip
Think back to the beginning of the play. What happens that John and Andrew do not expect?

6 Which sentence is the best summary of how the problem is resolved?

F Mr. Lopez says the boys can get a cat.

G Mrs. Lopez tells the boys to make posters.

H The girl and her father look for the kitten.

J The boys return the kitten to the girl.

TEKS RC-4(E)

Grade 4: Drama

Persuasive Text

Genre Overview

Persuasive text is a form of writing that presents information to influence what the reader thinks or does. The author of a persuasive text has a **purpose**, or reason, for writing. Usually, the author wants the reader to think or feel a certain way about a subject. This type of writing can include articles, letters, editorials, advertisements, or posters. Authors might also use special techniques, such as placing words and images together, to impact meaning. For example, an advertisement might include certain words that are bigger than other words on the page, or it might include pictures to catch the reader's attention.

Persuasive text is sometimes organized by cause-and-effect. A **cause** is the reason that something happens. An **effect** is what happens as a result. An example of cause and effect is *If a plant is watered, it will grow*. The cause is watering the plant. The effect is the plant's growth. Usually, authors of persuasive text will describe either a positive or negative effect in the process of arguing for or against a cause.

Persuasive text uses both facts and opinions. A **fact** is a statement that can be checked against an objective source to determine if it is true or false. An **opinion** *cannot* be proved true because it tells how a person feels about something. Persuasive text often uses opinions to try to persuade the reader.

Since language is an important part of persuasive text, be aware of new words as you read. Some of these words might be based on **Latin and Greek roots and affixes** (prefixes and suffixes). A **root** is the main part of a word. An **affix** is a set of letters attached to the beginning (prefix) or the end (suffix) of a root word. Affixes change a word's meaning. Use what you know about Latin and Greek words to help you understand the meaning of any new words that have these roots or affixes.

Grade 4: Persuasive Text

Name _____ Date _____

Persuasive Text

Read this selection. Then answer the questions that follow it.
Fill in the circle of the correct answer on your answer document.

Let's Change the Playground Now! *(handwritten: Q1)*

(handwritten: a really good school)

1   As a fourth-grade student at Dalton School, I would like to say that I am proud to be a part of this school. We have so many terrific teachers and good students. Mr. Stein is a hardworking, caring principal. We also have a wonderful playground at school and it is always fun to go outside at recess. However, as nice as the playground is, my classmates and I have a few suggestions to make it even better.

> **Tip**
>
> As you read, try to identify facts that can be proved and opinions that are the author's beliefs.

2   First, there is a jungle gym in the center of the school playground that students enjoy. Unfortunately, the jungle gym can get overcrowded and many students have to wait a long time to go on it. In addition, the swings are very popular, and everyone usually races to be the first one to get a swing. There are only four swings available on the swing set, so students often get left out. There should be a second structure added with swings attached to it. This will allow more students to get the chance to play on the equipment.

> **Tip**
>
> What is the strongest argument that the author makes about adding swings?

(handwritten: Q2 a popular place to play)

3   Second, there is a football field at the far end of the playground. We all love this field and really appreciate that the school added it a few years ago. Every day at recess, we create teams and play football games here. A lot of the time, other students come to watch us play. They would enjoy watching the football game much more if they had a place to sit. Adding bleachers to the football field would help to make it more comfortable to watch a

(handwritten: A dy football every day)

GO ON →

Grade 4: Persuasive Text

Name _____ Date _____

game. Also, it would be great to have bleachers as we start our new school football team this fall. We will have games after school and on weekends, and our parents and friends need a place to sit while they watch us.

4   Finally, the basketball court in the playground is not used enough. There is one tall hoop at each side of the court. I would like to suggest that you add a short hoop next to each tall hoop. Usually only the older and taller students play basketball because the younger and shorter students cannot get the ball in the hoop. If you add shorter hoops, everyone will want to play, and more students will use the basketball court.

it's not Populer

5   My classmates and I care about our school and want to make it enjoyable for everyone. We hope that you will make these changes to the playground as soon as possible. They will make a big difference in the lives of students here.

you should go to the schoole

Tip
Think about the language the author uses at the end of the passage to try to persuade readers.

GO ON ➡

1 The author wrote this passage to—

A explain how to play correctly on the jungle gym

B get more students to play in the playground

C encourage school leaders to make changes to the playground

D tell about the excellent teachers and principal of the school

TEKS 4.10

Tip
Reread paragraph 1 and think about the author's purpose.

2 In paragraph 2, the word structure comes from the Latin root *struere*, which means to—

F stop

G build

H need

J take

TEKS 4.2A

3 The author is concerned about the swings because—

A they are falling apart

B there are not enough of them

C they are not very popular

D there are broken seats

TEKS 4.11C

4 Which sentence from the passage best persuades readers to do what the author wants?

F *We have so many terrific teachers and good students.*

G *Mr. Stein is a hardworking, caring principal.*

H *This will allow more students to get the chance to play on the equipment.*

J *We all love this field and really appreciate that the school added it a few years ago.*

TEKS 4.12

Tip
Look for a sentence that relates directly to something the author wants.

5 Use the chart to answer the question below.

FACT	OPINION
There is a jungle gym in the center of the school playground. _____ _____ _____	It is always fun to go outside at recess. Students would enjoy watching football games more if they had a place to sit.

Which sentence belongs on the blank lines?

A Students have to wait too long to go on the jungle gym.

B The basketball court is not used enough by the students.

C If you add shorter hoops, everyone will want to play basketball.

D There are only four swings available on the swing set.

TEKS 4.11B

6 Which of the following would best support the author's purpose?

F A drawing of the playground with the author's suggestions

G An advertisement for a small, backyard playground

H A sign with the words "Dalton School Playground"

J An invitation to the author's birthday party

TEKS 4.14

Tip
Picture each of the answer choices and look for connections to what the author wants.

Grade 4: Persuasive Text

TEKS 4.2B, 4.3A, 4.4,
4.6B, 4.8, RC-4(D)

Poetry

Genre Overview

Poetry is a form of writing, often in rhyme, that tells a story or describes a person, place, feeling, or event. Poems are often divided into **stanzas**, or units with a fixed number of lines. A poem **rhymes** when two or more lines end with the same sound. A poet may use a pattern of line lengths, or line breaks, to create rhythm in a poem. **Rhythm** is the pattern of stressed and unstressed syllables in a line of poetry: BEAT the DRUM, and BLOW the HORN, for example.

Some poems have narrative structures like stories. These poems may also have characters that interact and develop. Some poems may also have a **theme**, or an underlying message that teaches the reader a lesson. For example, a theme might be *Treat others as you want to be treated*. A theme might be stated, but it usually requires you to infer it based on the details in the poem.

A poet might also use sensory language to help readers see, hear, or feel something in a poem, including similes and metaphors. **Similes** are comparisons that include the words *like* or *as*. **Metaphors** are comparisons that compare two things without using the words *like* or *as*.

Poets may sometimes use challenging vocabulary in their poems. Look for **context clues** in the poem if you see an unknown word, or a word that has **multiple meanings**. Often, the text surrounding that word will provide hints about the word's meaning.

Grade 4: Poetry

Poetry

TEKS 4.2B, 4.3A, 4.4,
4.6B, 4.8, RC-4(D)

> **Read this selection. Then answer the questions that follow it.**
> **Fill in the circle of the correct answer on your answer document.**

An Unwelcome Guest

1   A wild, gray guest blows into town
    And people pull their windows down.
    Rushing up and down the streets,
    It shoves at everyone it meets.

    We race inside and slam our doors.
6   The angry guest <u>shrieks</u> and roars.
    "This storm," we cry, "is more than rain!
    It has become a hurricane!"

    Denied our hospitality,
10 The guest tears through our fair city,
    It rips the branches off the trees
    And flings them in the street like skis.

    Its greenish clouds swirl and burst.
    Its manners are the very worst!
    It serves us rain—a watery dish.
16 Streets are streams and cars are fish.

    After putting out most every light
    And keeping us awake all night,
    The storm departs, a most rude guest,
20 Leaving us to clean its mess.

Tip

Notice how the poem rhymes
and uses rhythm.

Tip

Find the metaphor used in
line 16. Notice how this image
helps you understand the poem.

GO ON ➡

Grade 4: Poetry

Name _____ Date _____

1 How can you tell that "An Unwelcome Guest" is poetry?

A It includes dialogue.

B It is divided into stanzas.

C It has characters and a plot.

D It tells about important events in an author's life.

TEKS 4.4

2 What does the word shrieks mean in line 6?

F Laughs

G Asks

H Sings

J Screams

TEKS 4.2B

Tip
Use clues in the surrounding text to help you understand a word's meaning.

3 How do the residents of the city react to the "guest"?

A They fight against it.

B They welcome it.

C They run from it.

D They ask it to return.

TEKS 4.6B

4 Why does the poet compare cars to fish?

F To show that the cars are in water

G To show that the cars are blue

H To explain how cars can ride on water

J To explain why the cars are full of fish

TEKS 4.8

5 The poem includes a message about the—

A power of a storm

B need to work together

C excitement of a new adventure

D importance of fixing past mistakes

TEKS 4.3A

6

Inference	Text Evidence 1	Text Evidence 2
The storm is dangerous.	The storm rips branches off trees.	

Which of these belongs in the empty box?

F The storm blows into town.

G The storm leaves a mess.

H The storm has greenish clouds.

J The storm floods the city.

TEKS RC-4(D)

Grade 4: Poetry

Paired Selections

Genre Overview

Different kinds of texts can tell about the same topic. A **topic** is the subject of the text, or what the text is mostly about. A persuasive text might try to *convince* the reader to grow a garden. A procedural text might tell the reader *how* to grow a garden. The *topic* of both of these texts, though, is growing a garden.

After you have read two texts with the same topic, you can **make connections** between them. You might be asked to compare two **genres**, or kinds of texts, such as **poetry** and **expository text**, to find what is similar about them.

Poetry is a narrative form of writing that is typically divided into **stanzas**, or units. A poem may or may not **rhyme**, or have lines that end in the same sound. Patterns of line lengths, or **line breaks**, may create **rhythm** in a poem. Some poems have a **theme**, or overall lesson, that usually must be inferred.

Expository text gives facts and information about a topic. An expository text can be organized in several ways. One way is cause-and-effect. A **cause** is the reason something happens, such as an event or action. An **effect** is what happens as a result of the event or action.

Another way that expository text can be organized is by **sequence**. This means the writer gives information in a specific order. Some writers may use sequence to give **directions**, or steps in a process, for doing something.

Expository text can also be organized by **comparison**. The writer might describe different things, places, or events, and discuss their **similarities** (how they are the same) and their **differences** (how they are different).

Grade 4: Paired Selections

Read the next two selections. Then answer the questions that follow them.
Fill in the circle of the correct answer on your answer document.

The Rainy Picnic

1   We got to Green Tree Park,
    And found our favorite place.
    Mom stopped the car and gasped,
    As the smile left her face.

5   Dad and I looked out
    To see what caught Mom's eye.
    Above us there were dark, gray clouds,
    Filling up the sky.

    I said, "Let's not let this dark sky
10 Ruin our nice mood."
    So I opened up the basket,
    And handed out some food.

    As Dad munched on an apple,
    And watched the storm front grow,
15 He looked at us and said,
    "Let's just enjoy the show."

    The storm rained down in sheets.
    Its lightning burst all 'round.
    But no sooner had it started,
20 Than it left without a sound.

    We stepped out of the car,
    And all looked up together,
    To see a sky of blue,
    The perfect outdoor weather.

> **Tip**
>
> Notice that the word *face* rhymes with *place*. Look for other rhyming words as you read the poem.

> **Tip**
>
> Think about what Dad really means when he says, "Let's just enjoy the show."

GO ON

38

Paired Selections

TEKS 4.3A, 4.4, 4.11C, 4.13A, RC-4(F)

The Water Cycle

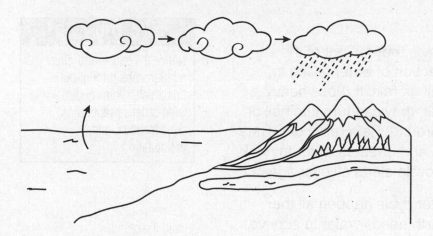

1   Water is in rainclouds and lakes. It is in trees and plants. Water comes out of the kitchen tap and the school fountain.

2   Water is always on the move. The movement of water is known as the *water cycle*. There are three steps in the water cycle: evaporation, condensation, and precipitation. Let's go through the steps one by one.

Evaporation

3   The water that is in ponds and rivers is a **liquid**. When water is heated up, it turns from a liquid to a gas. This gas is called **water vapor**. Water vapor is lighter than air, so it floats. When the sun heats liquid water to a certain temperature, water vapor floats up from places like oceans, lakes, and the surface of your skin. When water vapor gets up high in the air, it becomes much cooler than it was on the ground. This change in temperature starts the next step of the water cycle.

Condensation

4   **Condensation** happens when a gas changes to a liquid. When the water vapor reaches cold air, it turns back into liquid water. Air has many small bits of dust in it. When the water vapor cools, it condenses on the dust to form water droplets. The condensed water and dust eventually form clouds. The droplets join together and begin to form bigger drops, bringing us to the next step.

Tip

Use the headings to locate information and identify the main idea of each section.

Precipitation

5   When the droplets get heavy, they fall out of the clouds. **Precipitation** is the action of water falling to earth. Usually, water drops fall as rain. If those heavy drops fall through very cold air, they can turn into hail or snow before they reach the ground. Rain refills our rivers and lakes, helps plants grow, and gives us water to drink. After precipitation, the water cycle starts all over again.

6   The three steps of the water cycle happen all the time. Every living thing on earth needs water to survive, so we're lucky that the water cycle works so well. The next time you drink a glass of water, jump in a puddle, or look up at the clouds, remember the water cycle.

> **Tip**
>
> Notice the cause-and-effect relationships throughout this article. Think about what causes evaporation, condensation, and precipitation.

If you want to get a closer look at the water cycle in action, you can perform this evaporation experiment.

What you need:

• Water

• A plastic cup

• A marker

• A space near a sunny window

Directions:

1. Pour the water in the plastic cup.

2. Use the marker to draw a line where the top of the water is in the cup.

3. Set the cup in a space near a sunny window.

4. Wait 24 hours.

5. Check the cup of water.

Mark where the water level is now. There should be less water in the cup due to evaporation. The sun heated up the water and caused it to turn into vapor.

Name _____ Date _____

Use "The Rainy Picnic" to answer questions 1 and 2.

---

1 You can tell that "The Rainy Picnic" is poetry because it—

   A has a lesson or message

   B has lines that end with words that rhyme

   C gives directions that tell how to do something

   D includes a cast of characters and stage directions

TEKS 4.4

Tip
Think about the genre that is being described in each answer choice.

2 Which best describes a theme of the poem?

   F Sometimes you can fix a bad situation if you look at it differently.

   G Always prepare for the worst in case something goes wrong.

   H No one can control the weather, so don't even try.

   J It is important to spend time with your family.

TEKS 4.3A

Grade 4: Paired Selections

Use "The Water Cycle" to answer questions 3 and 4.

---

3 Use the chart to answer the question below.

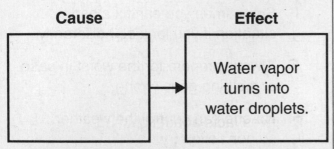

Cause	Effect
	Water vapor turns into water droplets.

Which of these belongs in the empty box?

A Water vapor reaches cold air.

B Water vapor changes to a gas.

C Water and dust form clouds.

D Water droplets join together.

TEKS 4.11C

4 In the directions for the evaporation experiment, what should you do after you mark the water level?

F Wait 24 hours.

G Find a plastic cup.

H Pour the water in the cup.

J Place the cup near a sunny window.

TEKS 4.13A

Tip
Reread the steps given for the evaporation experiment.

GO ON →

> **Use "The Rainy Picnic" and "The Water Cycle" to answer questions 5 through 8.**

5 Which step of the water cycle is described in "The Rainy Picnic"?

A Evaporation

B Water vapor

C Precipitation

D Condensation

TEKS RC-4(F)

Tip

Use the headings in "The Water Cycle" to find a description of each step.

---

6 Which step of the water cycle will begin after the rainstorm in "The Rainy Picnic"?

F Precipitation

G Condensation

H Water droplets

J Evaporation

TEKS RC-4(F)

7 A difference between the poem and the article is that the article—

A describes a personal experience

B explains how clouds form

C describes what happens during a rainstorm

D gives facts about lightning

TEKS RC-4(F)

Tip

After you read each answer choice, ask yourself if it applies to both the poem and the article, or just the article.

---

8 One idea in both the poem and the article is—

F it is nice to take a walk after a rainstorm

G the water cycle will always ruin a picnic

H water will evaporate if you leave it in a sunny window

J a step of the water cycle has a beginning and an end

TEKS RC-4(F)

> **Read this selection. Then answer the questions that follow it.**
> **Fill in the circle of the correct answer on your answer document.**

from **Piper Reed, Navy Brat**

by Kimberly Willis Holt

1   The empty townhouse smelled like fresh paint. And our words bounced off the bare walls.

2   "I have to share a room with Sam?" My old bedroom was twice this size, and I didn't have to share with anybody.

3   Mom frowned. "Well, someone has to share a room. There are only three bedrooms. It's only fair that Tori has her own room. She's the—"

4   "Oldest!" I said. "Why isn't there ever anything special for the middle child?"

5   Chief cleared his throat. "That's enough, Piper."

6   "I don't mind sharing a room," Sam said.

7   "Of course not," I said. "You're a scaredy-cat. You usually end up in Mom and Chief's bed anyway."

8   "Do not!"

9   "Do so!"

10   "Okay," said Chief. "The next person who speaks gets last place in the bathroom order." Then he added, "Permanently."

11   There was only one bathroom in the townhouse. Chief had already posted a list with bathroom orders plainly written out. Each day, the last person on the list rotated to the top. That way, every Reed had a turn to be first.

12   I'd started a list, too. My Why-I-Wish-We'd-Never-Moved list.

   1. I had my own room in San Diego.

   2. We had two bathrooms in our old house.

13   "Why can't we live in one of those big houses with the screen porches?" I asked.

Grade 4: Reading Practice

14   "That's the officers' housing," Chief said. "These homes are for <u>enlisted</u> families."

15   Mom's arm surrounded my shoulders and pulled me closer. "This is a nice home, Piper. Hey, where's that Gypsy spirit?"

16   I shrugged, but I wanted to say, *It's back in my tree house in San Diego.*

3. I had a tree house in San Diego.

17   I looked out the window at the backyard. This yard didn't even have a tree. It was almost too small for a swing set. What would keep Sam from pestering me?

18   Chief grabbed his keys. "Your mom and I need to get groceries from the commissary. Why don't y'all come along for the ride? We'll tour the base so you can see everything. We'll even drive by the beach."

19   "Can we go by my school?" Sam asked.

20   "You bet. The schools are <u>off-base</u>, so we'll check them out after we go to the commissary. Cheer up, girls. Besides, your mom and I have a surprise after dinner."

21   "Ice cream?" Sam asked.

22   "No. We have an announcement."

23   "What?" I asked.

24   "After dinner," Chief said.

25   I hated waiting for surprises. Every Christmas morning I woke up before the whole family just to see what everybody got before they did.

26   "Can't you tell us now?" Sam begged.

27   Chief winked. "You'll have to wait."

28   Walking to the van, Tori whispered to me. "I hope they're not having a baby."

29   "Why do you think that?" I asked.

30   "The last time they made a surprise announcement they told us we were moving here. So it's not that. The only other announcement they ever made was when they were expecting Sam. You don't remember because you were too little."

31   "I do, too, remember." But I was lying. I knew why Tori didn't want another sister or a brother though—so she wouldn't have to share her room with anyone.

Grade 4: Reading Practice

32   We drove around the base. It was a pretty base, as far as bases go. Palm trees and flowers grew in front of the chapel and the hospital. From the road, we could see the Gulf. The recreation area had a pool and some tennis courts. . . .

33   When we left my school, we drove by Tori's middle school. Then we headed back to the base. A few minutes later, we passed the gate guard, who motioned Chief onto the base. As we drove through, I thought about saluting him, but I got in trouble for doing that a long time ago when I was little. I *do* remember that.

34   Our furniture wouldn't arrive until tomorrow, so we ate on top of a blanket Mom had spread out on the living room floor. It was fun having a picnic indoors. Especially since we didn't have to worry about the ants.

35   After dinner, Chief said, "Here are your chore lists."

36   In a spooky voice, Mom said, "The list monster strikes again."

37   Chief rolled his eyes but handed out the lists anyway. Even Sam got one this time. She acted like it was really something big and started marching around the room, reading hers aloud.

38   "Sam's Chores. 1. Make your bed before breakfast. 2. Wipe off the table after each meal. 3. Dust the coffee table twice a week. 4.—"

39   "Was this the surprise announcement?" I asked, looking down at my chores.

40   "The lists?" Chief chuckled. "No. The surprise is something your mother and I have been discussing for a while now. We've decided this is the perfect time."

41   "Oh no," Tori muttered. "I knew it."

42   Tori better not get too comfortable staying in that room by herself.

43   We waited for them to say something. Chief wrapped his arm around Mom. "Your mother and I have decided we're going to let you have a dog."

Grade 4: Reading Practice

© Houghton Mifflin Harcourt Publishing Company

Name _____ Date _____

1 This story is an example of what genre?

A Fiction

B Nonfiction

C Drama

D Poetry

TEKS RC-4(D)

2 Why is it important to the plot that the Reed family is in the military?

F It explains why they have chores.

G It explains why they moved.

H It explains why Chief makes lists.

J It explains why Piper dislikes surprises.

TEKS RC-4(D)

3 From paragraph 11, the reader can tell that the—

A Reed sisters fight a lot

B Reed family does not like moving

C Reed sisters want a dog

D Reed family is very organized

TEKS RC-4(D)

4 Who tells this story?

F Chief

G Piper

H Tori

J A narrator

TEKS 4.6C

5 What lesson does Piper learn in the story?

A Things aren't always as bad as they seem.

B Be sure to speak up if you want something.

C Having sisters can cause problems.

D Always listen to your parents.

TEKS 4.3A

6 Which statement **BEST** describes how Piper changes in the story?

F She goes from disliking school to liking it.

G She goes from disliking dogs to liking them.

H She goes from disliking her new home to liking it.

J She goes from disliking the Navy to liking it.

TEKS 4.6B

GO ON

47

7 In paragraph 14, the word <u>enlisted</u>
means—

A not an officer

B not in the military

C too large

D new to the base

TEKS 4.2B

8 Use the chart to answer the question
below.

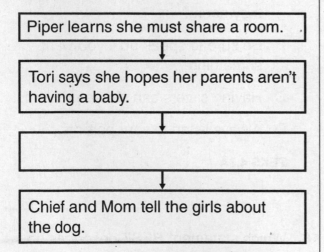

| Piper learns she must share a room. |
| Tori says she hopes her parents aren't having a baby. |
| |
| Chief and Mom tell the girls about the dog. |

Which belongs in the empty box?

F Chief posts a list of bathroom times.

G The Reed family tours the base
by car.

H Piper notices the size of the backyard.

J Piper creates her own list in her head.

TEKS 4.6A

9 In paragraph 20, <u>off-base</u> means—

A close to home

B in the center of the base

C close to the shopping centers

D away from the military base

TEKS 4.2B

10 Which is the best summary of the story?

F Piper does not like the new base and
plans to move back to her old home.

G Piper misses her old home, but she
starts to settle into her new home.

H Piper fights with her sisters over the
bathroom and does not like her new
school.

J Piper imagines what daily life will
be like in her new school and in her
new home.

TEKS RC-4(E)

Grade 4: Reading Practice

Read this selection. Then answer the questions that follow it.
Fill in the circle of the correct answer on your answer document.

What's So Great About . . .
GEORGE WASHINGTON CARVER

by Amie Jane Leavitt

1   As a child, George Washington Carver loved everything about nature. He saw things that other people didn't notice. George grew his own plants in a special place in the woods. He would take sick plants there to help them get better.

2   Soon, people heard about George's talent with plants. They called him the Plant Doctor. George was proud that people would call him such an important name.

GO ON

Helping the Farmers

3   One day, a famous African American named Booker T. Washington visited Carver. He wanted Carver to work at a school for African Americans called the Tuskegee Institute. Carver wouldn't make much money, but he would be able to teach people how to farm and take care of plants.

4   It wasn't long before Booker T. Washington knew he had made the right choice. He said that Carver was "a <u>great</u> teacher, a great lecturer, a great inspirer of young men and old men."

5   Carver knew that students learn best by trying things out for themselves. He once said, "The thoughtful educator realizes that a very large part of education must be gotten outside the four walls of the classroom." As much as possible, he took his students outdoors to study plants.

6   He also wanted to teach the local farmers how to grow better crops. A lot of farmers in the South were struggling to make money during this time period. Carver felt he could do something to help.

7   Most farmers in the South grew cotton. Before the Civil War, this crop had made people rich. Yet cotton was very hard on the soil. It removed all the nutrients. Soon, the cotton wouldn't grow anymore. The farmers had a hard time making any money to feed their families.

8   Carver taught the farmers that to build up the soil again, they needed to grow other things. He told them to grow peanuts.

9   The farmers just laughed at this. Why would they want to grow peanuts? Peanuts were not very popular. The farmers did not believe they could make much money growing them.

10   Carver believed differently. He knew that all plants were useful. He spent time in his <u>laboratory</u> to prove it. He did experiments on the peanuts. He wanted to find out how else they could be used.

11   One night, George invited the farmers to a feast. He prepared many delicious dishes. The farmers told George how much they loved the food. After everyone finished eating, George told them his secret. All the food was made from peanuts.

12   The farmers couldn't believe it! If peanuts were this useful, then maybe growing them would be a good idea after all.

GO ON

A Living Legacy

13   George Washington Carver wasn't just a scientist. He was also a musician and an artist. He could play the piano very well, and he was a talented painter. His specialty was painting nature pictures. He made his own paint colors using soil, rocks, and flower petals. He had other talents too. "I knit, I crochet, and made all my hose, mittens . . . while I was in school," he once told a friend.

14   Carver worked his entire life to help others. "Some day I will have to leave this world. And when that day comes, I want to feel that I have an excuse for having lived in it. I want to feel that my life has been of some service to my fellow man," he said in 1917.

15   Carver didn't care about riches. He took only a small salary from Tuskegee. He once said, "I've never received any money for my discoveries. Somebody who had benefited by one of my products from the peanut sent me $100 the other day, but I sent it back to him."

16   Carver dressed in old suits. "It is not the style of clothes one wears, neither the kind of <u>automobile</u> one drives, nor the amount of money one has in the bank, that counts. These mean nothing. It is simply service that measures success," he once said. Even though Carver dressed plainly, he always had a fresh flower pinned to his suit jacket.

17   Many important people had nice things to say about Carver. "Professor Carver has taken Thomas Edison's place as the world's greatest living scientist," said automaker Henry Ford near the end of Carver's life. In 1937, *Life* magazine named George "one of the great scientists of the U.S."

18   George Washington Carver died on January 5, 1943. When Franklin D. Roosevelt— President of the United States—heard the news, he was sad. "The world of science has lost one of its most eminent figures. All mankind," he said, would benefit from Carver's discoveries about plants and soil.

19   During his lifetime, George Washington Carver did many important things. He published books listing over 300 different uses for peanuts. He told people there were over 100 different ways to use the sweet potato. He helped farmers learn how to take better care of their land. He also helped Henry Ford learn how to use rubber from plants for car tires.

20   Carver never spent much money on himself, so he had a lot saved. In 1940, he used some of it to start the George Washington Carver Foundation. He left the rest of it to the Tuskegee Institute. This money helps people learn more about plants even today.

Grade 4: Reading Practice

Name _____ Date _____

1 George Washington Carver was a man who—

  A was only happy when he planted something

  B was never appreciated for his work

  C wanted to become a farmer

  D wanted to make a difference of some kind

  TEKS RC-4(D)

2 What is the meaning of <u>great</u> as used in paragraph 4?

  F Large in size

  G Large in number

  H Wonderful

  J Famous

  TEKS 4.2B

3 Which sentence shows that Carver hoped to help the people of the South?

  A *Carver knew that students learn best by trying things out for themselves.*

  B *As much as possible, he took his students outdoors to study plants.*

  C *He also wanted to teach the local farmers how to grow better crops.*

  D *The farmers had a hard time making any money to feed their families.*

  TEKS RC-4(D)

4 Read this dictionary entry for the word <u>laboratory</u>, as used in paragraph 10.

  > **laboratory** \ LAA-bruh-tor-ee \ *noun*
  > a place where scientific experiments are done

  Based on the dictionary entry, which syllable is stressed when pronouncing <u>laboratory</u>?

  F The first syllable

  G The second syllable

  H The third syllable

  J The fourth syllable

  TEKS 4.2E

5 Which sentence best shows that Carver did not care about money?

  A *"I want to feel that my life has been of some service to my fellow man,"he said in 1917.*

  B *"Somebody who had benefited by one of my products from the peanut sent me $100 the other day, but I sent it back to him."*

  C *Even though Carver dressed plainly, he always had a fresh flower pinned to his suit jacket.*

  D *Many important people had nice things to say about Carver.*

  TEKS RC-4(D)

GO ON ➡

Grade 4: Reading Practice

Name _____ Date _____

6 Which is the best summary of the section titled "Helping the Farmers"?

F Carver went to teach at the Tuskegee Institute. He taught students about plants. He also did a lot of experiments in his laboratory.

G While teaching at the Tuskegee Institute, Carver also taught local farmers how to grow a new kind of crop. He showed them that it is worthwhile to grow peanuts.

H Carver loved plants and made meals from what he grew. One night, he invited farmers to have a feast at his home. The entire meal was made of peanuts.

J Booker T. Washington asked Carver to work at a school for African Americans. Carver believed that students learn best by trying things out for themselves.

TEKS RC-4(E)

7 In paragraph 16, the word <u>automobile</u> comes from the Latin root *mobil*, which means to—

A build

B show

C move

D lift

TEKS 4.2A

8 Use the chart to answer the question below.

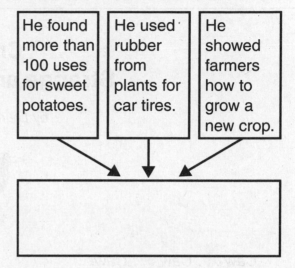

He found more than 100 uses for sweet potatoes.

He used rubber from plants for car tires.

He showed farmers how to grow a new crop.

Which of the following conclusions belongs in the empty box?

F Carver taught about plants at the Tuskegee Institute.

G Carver started the George Washington Carver Foundation.

H Carver was good at painting nature pictures.

J Carver used plants in new and creative ways.

TEKS RC-4(D)

Grade 4: Reading Practice

**Read this selection. Then answer the questions that follow it.
Fill in the circle of the correct answer on your answer document.**

Crows!
Strange and Wonderful

by Laurence Pringle

1   *Caw . . . Caw . . . Caw!*

2   A crow's voice is bold and sassy. Almost everyone has heard it.

3   We know crows by their calls. We know them by their large size—they are about twenty inches long—and by their glossy black feathers. Crows are not plain black, though. If you get close to a crow, you may see glints of deep blue and purple on its feathers.

4   Crows are often seen and heard, but to most people they are birds of mystery.

5   It is not easy to get close to crows. They are smart. They know that humans are sometimes their enemies. They manage to find safe places to <u>raise</u> their young, and they find food where millions of people live. You can often see crows hunting for food alongside roads, in parking lots and city parks, and on suburban lawns.

6   The crow you have most likely seen is the American or common crow. It lives in parts of every state, except Hawaii, and far north in Canada. The common crow has relatives all over the world. Its bird family, the *Corvidae*, includes rooks, jackdaws, magpies, and jays.

7   A smaller crow, the fish crow, lives in states along the Atlantic Coast and the Gulf of Mexico. Instead of "caw, caw," it calls out "car, car."

GO ON

Grade 4: Reading Practice

8   The largest member of the crow family is the common raven—a great dark bird of the Far North and of <u>rugged</u> mountaintops. Its call is a low, hoarse "quork, quork."

9   There is nothing "common" about the common raven and the common crow. The raven may be the smartest of all birds, as intelligent as a monkey. Other members of the crow family also have highly developed brains.

10   Crows show their intelligence in many ways. They are playful. Young crows may play tug-of-war with a twig. They swing upside down on tree branches. Sometimes a crow flies into the air with a stick in its beak, then drops it and swoops down to catch the stick before it hits the ground.

11   Crows tease other animals. Sometimes a crow gives a playful nip to the tail of a dog or other animal, then flies out of reach. Crows also mimic the calls of other birds. They imitate all sorts of other sounds—a squeaky door, a puppy's yelp, a cat's meow. Tame crows can be taught to say such words as "hello," "good-bye," and "hot dog."

12   Crows have a complex language. They make at least twenty-five different sounds. Besides cawing in many ways, they growl, squawk, squeal, coo, and rattle. By calling in different ways, a crow can identify itself to other crows, keep in touch with them, and say things to them.

13   A crow calling "Ko-ko, ko-ko, ko-ko" warns other crows to stay out of its territory. Calling "Caw, caw, caw" in a certain way warns other crows of danger—"Stay away!" Calling "Caw, caw, caw" in a different way has another meaning. For example, a series of quick, hoarse, drawn-out caws is the "assembly" call that urges other crows to come quickly.

14   Crows are always alert for animals that might be dangerous. They make scolding calls when a cat walks on the forest floor beneath their nest. But crows are most concerned about raccoons, foxes, large hawks, and large owls.

15   After dark, great-horned owls swoop through forests on silent wings, sometimes killing sleeping crows for food. When a crow spies a great-horned owl in the daytime, it gives the "assembly" call. Every crow within hearing distance hurries in, and a wild crow rumpus called "mobbing" begins.

Grade 4: Reading Practice

16   Cawing excitedly, dozens of crows perch or fly near the owl. Some crows may dart in to peck at its back. If the owl moves on its branch, the crow clamor grows louder. If the owl flies, trying to reach a safer hiding place, the crows become a roaring black cloud in pursuit.

17   People living near a crow roost complain about their noisy neighbors. Crows can be pests in other ways, too. Even one crow can damage a vegetable garden, and a large flock of crows can harm wheat, corn, and other farm crops.

18   Over the span of a year, however, crows eat many insects that harm crops, including wire worms, grasshoppers, cutworms, and weevils. Crows pluck beetle grubs (larvae) from the soil of lawns. Sometimes crows perch on cornstalks and peck at the tops of ripening ears of corn. They eat some corn, but they also eat corn earworms—insect larvae that have harmed the corn.

19   Crows can do harm, and they can do good. They are simply part of nature. They are fascinating creatures and are among the smartest and most adaptable birds on Earth.

20   *Caw . . . Caw . . . Caw!*

Grade 4: Reading Practice

© Houghton Mifflin Harcourt Publishing Company

1 What does the word <u>raise</u> mean as used in paragraph 5?

  A To lift higher

  B To take care of

  C To build

  D To collect

TEKS 4.2B

2 Based on its topic sentence, what is paragraph 6 most likely about?

  F Different types of crows

  G The common crow

  H Different birds in America

  J Birds that are common

TEKS 4.11D

3 According to the passage, how is a raven similar to a monkey?

  A Both have an "assembly" call.

  B Both live in the Far North.

  C Both can be taught to say words.

  D Both are very smart.

TEKS 4.11C

4 Read this dictionary entry for the word <u>rugged</u>.

> **rugged** \ RUHG-id \ *adjective*
> **1.** having a rough, rocky surface
> **2.** having a wrinkled face or appearance **3.** harsh or stern **4.** strong or tough

What is the definition of <u>rugged</u> as used in paragraph 8?

  F Definition 1

  G Definition 2

  H Definition 3

  J Definition 4

TEKS 4.2E

5 Which sentence from the passage is an opinion?

  A *Crows are often seen and heard, but to most people they are birds of mystery.*

  B *The common crow has relatives all over the world.*

  C *Besides cawing in many ways, they growl, squawk, squeal, coo, and rattle.*

  D *Sometimes crows perch on cornstalks and peck at the tops of ripening ears of corn.*

TEKS 4.11B

GO ON

Grade 4: Reading Practice

6 Use the chart to answer the question below.

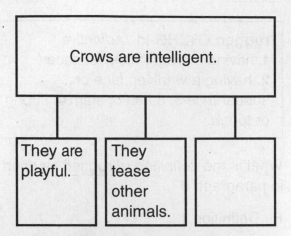

Crows are intelligent.

They are playful.

They tease other animals.

Which of the following details belongs in the empty box?

F They have glossy black feathers.

G They can cause a lot of damage.

H They eat insects that harm crops.

J They have a complex language.

TEKS 4.11A

7 The author wrote this passage to—

A entertain readers with a story about crows

B suggest that crows count on people to live

C remove some of the mysteries about crows

D tell the full history of crows

TEKS 4.10

8 Which is the best summary of this passage?

F Crows are smart animals. They show their intelligence by talking to each other with different sounds. People might think crows are noisy pests, but crows help people by eating insects that harm crops.

G Crows are bold and sassy. People do not like to see crows around. Crows search for food in parking lots and parks. Crows look black, but they actually have other colors in their feathers. There are different types of crows, and some are larger than others.

H Crows are extremely smart animals. They play by dropping a stick in mid-air and then catching it. They also like to tease other animals by nipping them and then flying away. Crows can imitate other animals, and they can even be taught to say words such as "hot dog."

J There are different kinds of crows, such as the common crow, the common raven, the magpie, and the jackdaw. Crows are smart and playful. They search for food in parking lots and on people's lawns. Crows can damage gardens and crops when there are a lot of them traveling together.

TEKS RC-4(E)

58

Read this selection. Then answer the questions that follow it.
Fill in the circle of the correct answer on your answer document.

Two Bear Cubs

adapted by Robert D. San Souci

Cast of Characters: STORYTELLER   MOTHER GRIZZLY   OLDER BROTHER
YOUNGER BROTHER   FOX   HAWK   MOUNTAIN LION   MEASURING WORM

Scene 1 *(Setting: A forest and mountain. Blue cloth across the front of the stage is a river. MOTHER GRIZZLY enters stage left, with OLDER BROTHER and YOUNGER BROTHER.)*

1   **OLDER BROTHER** *(Laughing and splashing):* Don't be afraid of a little water, Younger Brother!

2   **YOUNGER BROTHER** *(Splashing back):* I'm not, Older Brother!

3   **MOTHER GRIZZLY:** I want you to gather berries—but stay close and do not go downriver. Strange things happen there.

4   *(MOTHER GRIZZLY moves to stage left; the cubs move to stage right. A berry bush appears.)*

5   **OLDER BROTHER:** Look at these berries. *(He picks and eats them greedily.)* They are so sweet. Taste them!

6   **YOUNGER BROTHER:** We should take them to Mother.

7   **OLDER BROTHER:** Let's see what is downriver.

8   **YOUNGER BROTHER** *(Worried):* We are not supposed to go there.

9   **OLDER BROTHER** *(Taunting, starts off):* What is there to fear? *(After a moment's hesitation, YOUNGER BROTHER follows.)*

10   **YOUNGER BROTHER** *(Rubbing his eyes):* I'm tired. The hot sun and my full belly make me want to sleep.

11   **OLDER BROTHER** *(Yawning):* A nap would be good. *(A raised platform, decorated to look like a rock, slides into view.)*

GO ON

© Houghton Mifflin Harcourt Publishing Company

Grade 4: Reading Practice

12 **YOUNGER BROTHER** *(Pointing):* See that big, flat rock. It looks so warm. Let's rest there. *(The cubs lie down side by side, stretch, and fall asleep.)*

13 **STORYTELLER** *(Enters stage left):* The cubs fell asleep on the stone. But the stone was the seed of a mountain. As they slept, the stone grew, higher and higher . . . Meanwhile, Mother Grizzly wondered what had become of her cubs. *(Exits stage right)*

Scene 2 *(One hour later. MOTHER GRIZZLY enters stage left, calling.)*

14 **MOTHER GRIZZLY:** Older Brother! Younger Brother! *(MOTHER GRIZZLY sees Fox.)* Fox! Have you seen my cubs?

15 **FOX:** No. I have been building a new home.

16 **MOTHER GRIZZLY** *(Cups paws around her mouth and shouts up to HAWK):* Hawk! Have you seen my cubs?

17 **HAWK** *(Calling down):* They are asleep on this strange new mountain.

18 **MOTHER GRIZZLY:** Please fly to my children! Wake them, and help them find their way down.

19 *(HAWK pantomimes flying toward cubs and being blown back by mountain winds.)*

20 **HAWK** *(Calling down):* The wind will not let me. Someone will have to climb up and rescue them.

21 **STORYTELLER** *(Enters stage left):* One by one, the animals tried to reach the cubs, but none could. Even Mountain Lion failed. *(Exits stage right)*

22 *(MOTHER GRIZZLY begins to weep. The other creatures gather around to <u>console</u> her. Unnoticed by them, MEASURING WORM enters.)*

23 **MOTHER GRIZZLY** *(Sadly):* Mountain Lion, you are the best climber and were my best hope. There is no one now who can save my cubs.

24 **MEASURING WORM:** I will try.

25 *(The other animals turn and stare at him, and then all except MOTHER GRIZZLY begin to laugh.)*

Scene 3 *(One hour later. STORYTELLER enters stage right.)*

26 **STORYTELLER:** In time Measuring Worm climbed even higher than Mountain Lion, all the while crying—

27 **MEASURING WORM:** Tu-tok! Tu-tok! Tu-tok!

Grade 4: Reading Practice

28   *(STORYTELLER exits as MEASURING WORM bends over the two sleeping cubs and calls—)*

29   **MEASURING WORM:** Wake up!

30   **OLDER BROTHER** *(Crawls and looks over the side of the rock):* Younger Brother! Something terrible has happened. Look how high we are.

31   **YOUNGER BROTHER** *(Also on his knees, peers down):* We are trapped here. We will never get back to our mother. *(The cubs begin to cry.)*

32   **MEASURING WORM** *(Comforting the cubs):* Do not be afraid. I have come to guide you safely down the mountain. Just follow me, and do as I say.

33   **FOX** *(Excitedly, pointing to a spot about halfway up the mountain):* Mother Grizzly, look! Measuring Worm is guiding your cubs down the mountain.

34   *(All the animals look where Fox is pointing.)*

35   **MOTHER GRIZZLY** *(Joyful, fearful):* Be careful!

36   *(The animals watch the climbers. The cubs and MEASURING WORM make a final leap from the mountain to the ground. The cubs run to their mother. MOTHER GRIZZLY gives them a big hug. Then she shakes her finger at them.)*

37   **MOTHER GRIZZLY** *(Scolding):* Both of you have been very naughty! Look at the trouble and worry you have caused us all.

38   **OLDER BROTHER** *(Hanging head):* I'm sorry. I won't do it again.

39   **YOUNGER BROTHER** *(Starting to cry):* I will never disobey you again.

40   **MOTHER GRIZZLY** *(Gathering them up in her arms again):* But do not cry, little ones. It has all ended well, thanks to the help and courage of Measuring Worm.

41   *(The animals gather around MEASURING WORM and congratulate him.)*

42   **STORYTELLER** *(Enters stage left):* Then all the animals decided to call the new mountain Tu-tok-a-nu-la, which means "Measuring Worm Stone." This was to honor the heroic worm who did what no other creature could do.

Grade 4: Reading Practice

Name _____ Date _____

1 How do you know that this selection is a drama?

A It has a plot.

B It has characters.

C It has stage directions.

D It has a theme.

TEKS RC-4(D)

2 Who are the three main characters?

F Hawk, Fox, Mountain Lion

G Storyteller, Hawk, Measuring Worm

H Storyteller, Older Brother, Younger Brother

J Mother Grizzly, Older Brother, Younger Brother

TEKS 4.6B

3 What event introduces the problem in the drama?

A Older Brother leads Younger Brother downriver..

B The animals laugh at Measuring Worm.

C Hawk sees the cubs on the mountain.

D Measuring Worm finds the cubs.

TEKS 4.6A

4 The stage direction *Enters stage left* means the actor enters from the—

F audience's left

G audience's right

H back

J audience

TEKS 4.5

5 Use the following diagram to answer the question.

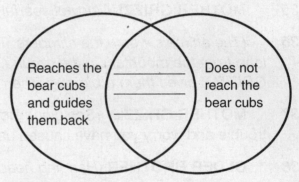

Measuring Worm   **Mountain Lion**

Reaches the bear cubs and guides them back   _____   Does not reach the bear cubs

Which of these belongs on the blank lines?

A Is feared by other animals

B Is afraid of high places

C Is a great swimmer

D Is a great climber

TEKS 4.6B

GO ON

Grade 4: Reading Practice

6 Which of the following is not a stage direction?

F *Setting: A forest and mountain.*

G **MEASURING WORM:** I will try.

H *(Yawning)*

J *(He picks and eats them greedily.)*

TEKS 4.5

7 In paragraph 9, the word <u>hesitation</u> means—

A trembling in fear

B pausing before moving

C arguing

D agreeing

TEKS 4.2B

8 How do the animals change in Scene 3?

F They go from liking Measuring Worm to disliking him.

G They go from laughing at Measuring Worm to honoring him.

H They go from liking Mother Grizzly to disliking her.

J They go from wanting to help Mother Grizzly to giving up.

TEKS 4.6B

9 In paragraph 22, the word <u>console</u> means—

A try to make angry

B try to make feel better

C give advice to

D criticize

TEKS 4.2B

10 Which of these is the best summary of the drama?

F Two cubs go off to gather berries. They fall asleep on a rock. The rock rises up into a mountain. All the animals try to rescue the cubs.

G Two cubs wander away and get lost. They fall asleep on a magic mountain. Mother Grizzly scolds them for disobeying her.

H Two cubs disobey Mother Grizzly and wander off. They get trapped on a mountaintop. Measuring Worm saves the cubs and earns the respect of all the animals.

J A rock turns into a mountain. None of the animals except Measuring Worm can climb to the top. The animals name the new mountain in honor of Measuring Worm.

TEKS RC-4(E)

Grade 4: Reading Practice

Name _____   Date _____

Reading
PRACTICE

TEKS 4.2A, 4.2B, 4.2E,
4.11B, 4.12, 4.14A, 4.14B,
4.14C, RC-4(D)

> **Read this selection. Then answer the questions that follow it.**
> **Fill in the circle of the correct answer on your answer document.**

Protect the Manatees

1   Manatees are harmless water mammals, also known as "sea cows." These gentle giants have thick, rounded bodies and paddle-shaped tails. Their faces are wrinkled, and they have whiskers on their snouts. Manatees look a lot like walruses, but without the tusks. They are very large creatures. Adult manatees can grow to be 12 feet long and weigh up to 1,200 pounds. They swim slowly near the shore, eating sea grass and other <u>plants</u>. Adults can eat up to 150 pounds of food a day!

2   Manatees are endangered animals. There are fewer than 5,000 manatees in the United States. These animals are in danger of disappearing forever. One reason is that they can only survive in certain habitats, such as the warm, shallow waters around Florida and in the Gulf of Mexico. Another reason manatees are in danger is that their population grows very slowly. Females usually give birth to only one baby every two to five years.

3   Manatees are also endangered by humans. Speedboats are the manatee's greatest enemy. Manatees swim slowly, close to the surface of the water. The blades of a fast-moving motorboat can cause serious injury or death to these creatures. Humans also make the water in manatee habitats less clean. <u>Pollution</u> can make manatees sick, further threatening their survival.

4   We must do something to help manatees. There are ways that people can keep these innocent animals safe. Drivers of fast-moving boats do not see manatees until it is too late. Therefore, slow-speed zones in areas where manatees live would help to protect them. A poster, such as the one on the next page, could be displayed on the waterways where manatees live.

Name _____ Date _____

Reading
PRACTICE

TEKS 4.2A, 4.2B, 4.2E,
4.11B, 4.12, 4.14A, 4.14B,
4.14C, RC-4(D)

SLOW DOWN TO SAVE THE MANATEES!

You are passing through the habitat of the manatee.

Manatees are **ENDANGERED** partly due to motorboat injuries.

Please respect these creatures by doing the following:

- **SLOW DOWN!**

  Give manatees time to get out of your way. Slow-moving propellers are less likely to hurt a manatee.

- **WATCH OUT!**

  Keep a lookout for manatees while driving through their habitat. If you see a manatee, turn your boat to avoid hitting it.

- **BE CLEAN!**

  Do not throw any garbage or food into the water. This pollution can make manatees very sick.

  There are only a few thousand manatees left in the United States.

  Do your part to keep these beautiful creatures alive!

  THANK YOU!

Grade 4: Reading Practice

Name _____   Date _____

Reading
PRACTICE

TEKS 4.2A, 4.2B, 4.2E,
4.11B, 4.12, 4.14A, 4.14B,
4.14C, RC-4(D)

5   Another idea is for boaters to place propeller guards on the boats they <u>operate</u>. These guards help to protect the manatees in case a boat hits them. If boat operators use these guards and drive more slowly, they will give manatees a better chance to survive.

6   People can also protect the water where manatees live. They can limit construction on nearby land, and reduce chemicals that run into the water. These chemicals pollute the water, making the manatees' habitats unsafe.

7   Protecting manatees today is important for the species to survive tomorrow. If we do not want to see this animal disappear, we must act immediately. We must urge boaters to slow down and put guards on their propellers. We must also remind people to keep manatee habitats clean and safe from pollution. We also need to stop developing land near the manatees' habitats. If everyone educates just one other person about saving the manatees, we may be able to ensure that these interesting and gentle creatures will be around for a long time.

1 What does the word <u>plants</u> mean as used in paragraph 1?

   A Factories or businesses used to build and make things

   B Living things that grow and are often used as food

   C Puts in the ground for the purpose of growing

   D Places down with great force or firmness

TEKS 4.2B

2 Read this dictionary entry for the word <u>pollution</u> in paragraph 3.

> **pollution** \ puh-LOO-shun \ *noun*
> the introduction of harmful things into an environment

Based on the dictionary entry, how many syllables are in the word <u>pollution</u>?

   F One

   G Two

   H Three

   J Four

TEKS 4.2E

3 Use the chart to answer the question below.

FACT	OPINION
Manatees have whiskers on their snouts.	We must help manatees.
Manatees only live in certain places.	_____

Which of these belongs on the blank line?

   A Protecting manatees is important.

   B Pollution makes manatees sick.

   C Manatees are found in the Gulf of Mexico.

   D Manatees swim close to the water's surface.

TEKS 4.11B

4 The poster's main goal is to make boaters feel—

   F disappointed

   G nervous

   H angry

   J responsible

TEKS 4.14B

Grade 4: Reading Practice

Name _____ Date _____

5 The word "endangered" is capitalized and bold in the poster to—

A tell about the history of manatees

B help explain the poster's tips

C point out how serious the issue is

D give a definition of the word

TEKS 4.14A

6 How is the language in the poster different from the language in the rest of the passage?

F It asks interesting questions that the passage does not address.

G It includes stronger words to persuade the reader to do something.

H It gives helpful suggestions about how readers can do their part.

J It uses a pleasant tone to urge readers to help the manatees.

TEKS 4.14C

7 In paragraph 5, the word <u>operate</u> comes from the Latin root *oper*, which means—

A work

B take

C think

D learn

TEKS 4.2A

8 Which best describes how propeller guards help manatees?

F They cover sharp blades on boats.

G They force boaters to slow down.

H They warn manatees of where the boats are.

J They push manatees out of a boat's path.

TEKS RC-4(D)

9 Read the following sentence from paragraph 7.

> *If we do not want to see this animal disappear, we must act immediately.*

The author uses this sentence to—

A make the reader want to create posters

B make the reader feel that time is running out

C suggest that there is no hope for the manatees

D suggest that the manatees do not need help

TEKS 4.12

68

**Read this selection. Then answer the questions that follow it.
Fill in the circle of the correct answer on your answer document.**

The Women's Team at L. Bamberger & Co.

by Lillian Morrison

1   Our best <u>forward</u>
    wasn't very tall
    but made up for it
    in speed, spunk and

5   spring in the knees.
    She could almost slam-dunk.
    Proud, in our <u>snazzy</u>
    silver shorts, maroon tops,
    we ran and sweated

10   in those drafty gyms
    (seats mostly empty)
    somehow always playing
    against bigger, rougher teams,
    tough girls who shoved

15   and elbowed, but Maggie's
    fakes and pivots, charges
    down the floor, layups,
    jumpers, onehanders
    would fire us up, and the

20   few times we did win,
    the bare locker rooms,
    as we showered and dressed,
    rang with our rejoicing
    and when we <u>emerged</u>, heading

25   for the bus, each of us
at least two inches taller,
the frosty air outside
seemed to greet us with kisses.

GO ON

1 Who is speaking in the poem?

A Maggie

B A spectator

C L. Bamberger & Co.

D A team member

TEKS 4.6C

2 Read this entry for the word <u>forward</u>.

> **forward** \ FAWR-werd \ *adverb*
> onward or ahead; *adjective* ready or
> eager; *noun* a player on a team; *verb*
> to advance

What part of speech is the word <u>forward</u>
as used in line 1?

F Adverb

G Adjective

H Noun

J Verb

TEKS 4.2E

3 What does <u>snazzy</u> mean in line 7?

A Dark

B Flashy

C Wrinkled

D Stringy

TEKS 4.2B

4 Use the web to answer the question
below.

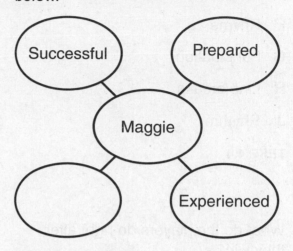

Which of these belongs in the
empty circle?

F Angry

G Honest

H Talented

J Responsible

TEKS 4.6B

5 How do Maggie's actions affect those of
her teammates?

A They make her teammates feel better
when they lose.

B They show her teammates that she
should be the captain.

C They get her teammates angry at the
other team.

D They make her teammates want to
win the game.

TEKS 4.6A

GO ON →

Grade 4: Reading Practice

6 Which of the following is something the poet does NOT use?

F Rhyme

G Punctuation

H Line breaks

J Rhythm

TEKS 4.4

7 What do the players do right after they win?

A They get fired up.

B They go to the locker room.

C They get on the bus.

D They run in the drafty gym.

TEKS 4.6A

8 Which best describes the message of the poem?

F Respect your elders.

G Victory is sweet.

H Winning isn't everything.

J Learn from your mistakes.

TEKS 4.3A

9 How can you tell that "The Women's Team at L. Bamberger & Co." is poetry?

A It includes stage directions.

B It gives facts and details about a topic.

C It is divided into stanzas.

D It has characters and a plot.

TEKS 4.4

10 What does the word emerged mean in line 24?

F Came out

G Sat down

H Hugged

J Entered

TEKS 4.2B

11 The team is described as being two inches taller at the end of the poem to show—

A that they still wore their sneakers when they left

B that each player had gotten older at the game

C how they thought they needed to be bigger

D how proud they were that they had won

TEKS 4.8

STOP

Name _____ Date _____

Reading
PRACTICE

TEKS 4.2B, 4.4, 4.8, 4.11C,
4.13A, 4.13B, RC-4(D),
RC-4(E), RC-4(F)

> **Read the next two selections. Then answer the questions that follow them.**
> **Fill in the circle of the correct answer on your answer document.**

On the Way to Californ-I-A!

by Bobbi Katz

1   Year after year, the land was dry.
We prayed for rain,
watched crops shrivel and die.

Then the winds started blowing,
5   and the sky turned bloodred.
But no raindrops fell.
It rained red dust instead.

The sun disappeared.
Day turned into night.
10   We rushed inside.
Tried to make the house tight.

And the terror winds blew and blew and blew.
And the terror winds blew and blew.

"There's jobs in Californ-I-A!"
15   That's what Pa says some folks say.
So we loaded our jalopy,
and we're on our way today!

On our way to Californ-I-A
where oranges,
20   tomatoes,
and potatoes grow,
and where
terror winds don't *ever* blow.
No, the terror winds don't blow.

GO ON

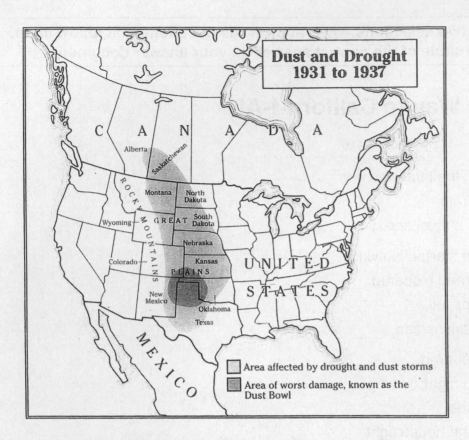

Dust and Drought
1931 to 1937

□ Area affected by drought and dust storms
■ Area of worst damage, known as the
Dust Bowl

from *Children of the Dust Days*

by Karen Mueller Coombs

Black Blizzards

1   No rain! Year after year, no rain! Ponds dried up. Soil cracked.
Drought gripped the plains of North America. Between 1931 and 1937,
the dry land spread from Texas to the prairies of Canada. Life there
became hard for children and their parents.

2   When a bit of rain fell, crops sprouted. Then grasshoppers came.
They munched the new plants down to the ground. Sometimes the
'hoppers even ate the wash drying on the line.

3   With no rain, few seeds sprouted. No roots grew to hold the earth
in place. Wind lifted the soil from the dry, plowed fields. The wind flung
the soil across the land. Billowing dust clouds looked like black
blizzards. The soil sometimes blew all the way to the Atlantic Ocean.
It drifted down on ships at sea.

Name _____ Date _____

Reading
PRACTICE

TEKS 4.2B, 4.4, 4.8, 4.11C,
4.13A, 4.13B, RC-4(D),
RC-4(E), RC-4(F)

4   People could see the dust clouds coming. Town children quickly gathered their marbles and balls and headed home. Farm children helped herd animals into the barn.

5   Dust storms were dangerous. It was hard to breathe. Dust seeped into lungs and made children spit up dirt. Too much dust in the lungs could cause illness—sometimes death.

6   Getting lost in the blinding dust was easy. Children who lost their way might smother. So, as soon as they could, boys and girls scurried indoors when the wind started to blow.

7   Inside, everyone helped cram rags and towels into the cracks around doors and windows. This didn't stop all the dust. Ann said the air in her house was "just a haze." Her family covered their faces with wet rags. Roxanne "choked on the dust and had to use a damp cheesecloth smeared with Vicks to breathe through."

8   Water was scarce during the drought. After washing hands and faces, people saved the water to scrub clothes. Only then did they use it to clean floors.

9   On farms, children helped dig out buried equipment. They rescued half-buried chickens and pigs. They cleaned gritty dust out of cows' nostrils.

10   Fence posts needed to be raised. Then the next storm wouldn't bury the fences and make them useless. Children tried not to touch metal while working. Right after a storm, static electricity filled the air. ZAP! Metal gave a strong shock.

11   After chores, children had fun searching for arrowheads. They were easier to find with the topsoil <u>scoured</u> away.

12   Year after year, the dust flew. Even when no wind blew, fine dust hung in the air, sifting down like dirty flour. The plains of North America had become a huge field of dust. One area was even drier and dustier than the rest. People called that area the Dust Bowl. The dust buried towns, farms, wagons, trucks, and animals. It buried people's hopes and dreams.

Dust Days Clothing

How to Make a Burlap Shirt

13   People often didn't have enough money for new clothes during the days of the dust storms. Back then, flour was packaged in cotton sacks. Crop seeds and feed for animals came in large sacks made from burlap, a rough, scratchy, brown fabric. When the sacks were empty, mothers washed them and used them to make clothes. The sacks did not make very stylish clothing, but it was better than nothing at all.

GO ON

Burlap Shirt

flexible tape measure
½ yard burlap (approximate) per child*
black magic marker
scissors
2 safety pins
yarn
large-eyed, blunt-end needle

*Widths for burlap vary, but you should have a rectangle of cloth.

1. Using a flexible tape measure, measure the distance from the tip of one shoulder to the tip of your other shoulder. Spread the rectangle of burlap flat, so a long edge is facing you. Place the tape measure on top of the fabric, starting at one edge. Use a magic marker to mark off the span of your shoulders. Repeat, marking in the middle and at the other edge.

2. Use a scissors to cut in a straight line from one marking to the next, removing the excess fabric.

3. Fold the short ends of fabric together. To make a neck opening, make a small snip with the scissors in the center of the fold. Then enlarge the snip, cutting from the center along the fold approximately 4 inches in either direction.

4. For armholes, measure 6 inches below the fold on each side. Secure the fabric below each armhole with a safety pin.

5. Measure 3 feet of yarn. Thread the yarn through a large-eyed, blunt-end needle. Knot the yarn end. Sew one side seam of the shirt, starting at the bottom of one armhole and ending at the bottom edge of the shirt. Keep your sewing to within ½ to 1 inch of the fabric edge. Knot the end of the yarn. Repeat your sewing on the opposite edge. Remove the safety pins. Turn your shirt inside out if desired.

6. Wear the shirt next to your skin for as long as you can stand it.

Name _____ Date _____

Reading
PRACTICE

TEKS 4.2B, 4.4, 4.8, 4.11C,
4.13A, 4.13B, RC-4(D),
RC-4(E), RC-4(F)

Use "On the Way to Californ-I-A!" to answer questions 1 through 4.

---

1 You can tell that "On the Way to Californ-I-A!" is poetry because it—

A has a lesson or message

B has lines that end with words that rhyme

C gives directions that tell how to do something

D includes a cast of characters and stage directions

TEKS 4.4

2 What does the narrator mean when she writes "And the terror winds blew and blew and blew"?

F The rain fell so fast that it appeared to be blue.

G The wind was afraid of the dust storms, too.

H It sounded like a flock of birds when the wind blew.

J The winds were scary and they blew all the time.

TEKS 4.8

3 Which line from the poem shows that the narrator is excited to be moving to California?

A *Then the winds started blowing,*

B *But no raindrops fell.*

C *That's what Pa says some folks say.*

D *and we're on our way today!*

TEKS RC-4(D)

4 Which is the best summary of the poem?

F The land is dry for a few years. Then the wind blows and the narrator and her family rush inside. They try to stay away from the wind.

G The narrator's family copes with a drought that causes crops to die and dust storms. Then they hear that California has jobs and crops, so they decide to move there.

H Crops shrivel and die. The narrator's family misses oranges, tomatoes, and potatoes, so they talk about moving to California.

J Red dust rains down from the sky. The narrator is afraid of the wind, so she tries to make the house tight. Her father says that California has jobs and crops.

TEKS RC-4(E)

GO ON

Grade 4: Reading Practice

Name _____ Date _____

Reading
PRACTICE

TEKS 4.2B, 4.4, 4.8, 4.11C,
4.13A, 4.13B, RC-4(D),
RC-4(E), RC-4(F)

Use the excerpt from *Children of the Dust Days* to answer questions 5 through 8.

5 In paragraph 11, the word <u>scoured</u> means—

A rubbed

B piled

C darkened

D screamed

TEKS 4.2B

6 Use the chart to answer the question below.

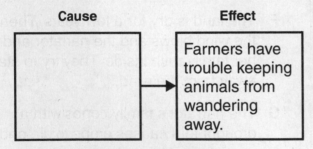

Cause	Effect
	Farmers have trouble keeping animals from wandering away.

Which of these belongs in the empty box?

F Dust storms bury the fences that contain the animals.

G Wind from the storm drives the animals to another farm.

H Animals get scared by the grasshoppers and run away.

J Farmers feed their families before feeding the animals.

TEKS 4.11C

7 Which state included the area known as the Dust Bowl?

A Nebraska

B Texas

C Montana

D California

TEKS 4.13B

8 Refer to the directions for making a burlap shirt. Where would you add this new step?
Cut the extra yarn from the shirt.

F After Step 1

G After Step 2

H After Step 4

J After Step 5

TEKS 4.13A

GO ON

Grade 4: Reading Practice

Name _____ Date _____

Reading
PRACTICE

TEKS 4.2B, 4.4, 4.8, 4.11C,
4.13A, 4.13B, RC-4(D),
RC-4(E), RC-4(F)

> **Use "On the Way to Californ-I-A!" and the excerpt from *Children of the Dust Days*
> to answer questions 9 through 12.**

9 Which line from "On the Way to Californ-I-A!" best describes what would happen when a "black blizzard" came?

A *Year after year, the land was dry*.

B *But no raindrops fell*.

C *Day turned into night*.

D *No, the terror winds don't blow*.

TEKS RC-4(F)

10 In "On the Way to Californ-I-A!" the narrator's family tried "to make the house tight" to—

F keep the dust out of the house

G grow oranges inside of the house

H make sure the animals did not escape

J prevent grasshoppers from getting inside

TEKS RC-4(F)

11 Based on both of these passages, you can tell that California—

A did not have any wind

B was the only place in the country that had jobs

C was where all oranges, tomatoes, and potatoes grew

D did not have the same problems as the Dust Bowl states

TEKS RC-4(F)

12 Both passages show that people who experienced the drought—

F liked to wear burlap shirts

G got lost in the dust storms

H had to work hard to survive

J ate oranges during the storms

TEKS RC-4(F)

© Houghton Mifflin Harcourt Publishing Company

Grade 4: Reading Practice

Writing a One-Page Composition

Responding to a Prompt

Do you ever write in a journal? Do you use email? Do you write reports for school? You probably answered *yes* to at least one of these questions. If so, you know that people use writing every day. That is why it is important to know how to write well. Writing well means:

- Focusing on one personal experience or central idea
- Organizing your writing in a logical way
- Developing your ideas with specific details and examples

On a test, you will be given a writing prompt. The prompt will ask you to write a one-page personal narrative or a one-page expository composition. The prompt will include rules to follow when you write. These rules are **READ** or **LOOK, THINK,** and **WRITE.** Read the prompt carefully to make sure you understand it.

Step 1: Plan Your Composition

It is very important to organize your ideas before you start writing. Think about these examples:

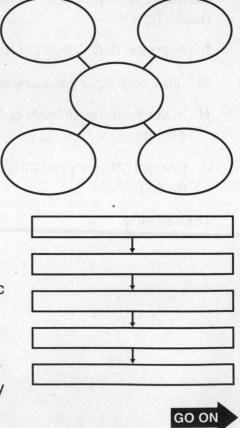

- A prompt asks you to write a one-page personal narrative about an important event in your life. On a separate sheet of paper, you can draw a web such as the one at right. First write the important event in the center circle. Then list ideas and details about the event in the other circles. Decide which details to keep, and cross out the rest. Once you finish your web, you are ready to write a first draft of your personal narrative. Remember that your composition can be no longer than one page.

- Another prompt asks you to write a one-page expository composition explaining how to do something. You can use a flowchart such as the one at right. At the top of the flowchart, write a topic sentence to establish your **central idea.** Then list each step or detail in your explanation in the boxes of the flowchart. Make sure your steps follow a logical order and connect to your central idea. Now you are ready to write a first draft of your expository composition.

GO ON

Step 2: Draft Your Composition

You can use the ideas in your graphic organizer to write a first draft. You should have a clear beginning, middle, and ending. Develop your ideas by using specific details and well-chosen examples. Be sure to reread the writing prompt and check that you have responded to it correctly.

Step 3: Revise and Edit Your Composition

Reread your draft to make sure that you have responded correctly to the writing prompt. Look for ways to improve your writing. For example:

- As you reread your personal narrative, look for sentences that do not focus on the event you discussed. Delete sentences that do not tell about that event, and add sentences that do.

- As you reread your expository composition, delete or rewrite sentences that do not support the central idea. Check that every fact, detail, and explanation is specific and connects to the central idea. Make sure that you have a strong concluding statement at the end of your composition.

- For each type of composition, ask yourself questions like these:
  - Does every sentence have a purpose? If not, delete or rewrite them.
  - Are all my sentences in the best places? If not, consider moving them around.
  - Does my writing seem choppy? Think about varying the lengths of the sentences.
  - Does my writing flow smoothly? Is it easy to understand? If not, consider where you could add transition words, such as *next, then, as a result,* to connect your ideas clearly.

- When you are writing a one-page composition, every sentence counts and every word counts. Look again at your word choices. Replace overused words with words that are more interesting and descriptive. Delete any words that are not necessary.

- Now check your draft for errors in language conventions. Correct errors in spelling, grammar, capitalization, and punctuation. Errors like these can distract and confuse readers.

- **Your final draft should include all of the changes you made.** Write neatly so readers can understand every word. Make sure your composition is no longer than one page.

Name _____ Date _____

Written Composition: Personal Narrative

READ

Read the story in the box below.

> Elena wanted to play on the school's basketball team. Tryouts were early in the fall, so she spent every day of her summer vacation practicing with her father. By the end of the summer, she had become a better player. When tryouts came, Elena did her best and made it on the team. She worked hard and reached her goal.

THINK

Think of a goal you have had and why it was important to you. Then think about what you did to achieve this goal.

Tip

Before you begin writing, list the steps you took to achieve your goal.

WRITE

Write a one-page personal narrative about a time you worked to achieve a goal that was important to you.

As you write your composition, remember to —

❑ describe a personal experience—a time you worked to achieve an important goal.

❑ organize your ideas in an order that makes sense, and connect ideas using transitions.

❑ develop your ideas with details that help readers understand your experience and your feelings.

❑ use correct spelling, capitalization, punctuation, grammar, and sentences.

❑ make sure your composition is no longer than one page.

Tip

When you have finished your draft, make sure each word is well chosen and each sentence serves your purpose.

82

Sample Response: Personal Narrative

> Write a one-page personal narrative about a time you worked to achieve a goal that was important to you.

The writer describes the goal and how he or she worked toward it.

The writer uses the pronouns I and my to show the first-person point of view.

All week long I was on my best behavior. If I did all my chores around the house, my parents said I could have a birthday party and invite ten friends over.

Let me tell you, it wasn't easy. Washing sticky plates and taking out trash that smelled like dead fish was no fun. But Friday was my last day of chores, so I got dressed quickly and hurried down to the kitchen.

"Are you ready to walk Max?" Mom asked. Max is my St. Bernard. He weighs seventy-five pounds. He was waiting for me by the door with his leash in his mouth. I put the leash on him and walked him very carefully around the block.

Thank goodness, he decided to be a good dog that day. Sometimes he likes to chase cars. When I got back to the house, my parents were waiting for me. They were both smiling. Mom and Dad said together, "Congratulations!"

I couldn't believe it. The week was over, and I had done it. I was going to have my big birthday party. Hooray!

Grade 4: Personal Narrative

Sample Response: Personal Narrative

> Write a one-page personal narrative about a time you worked to achieve
> a goal that was important to you.

A goal that was important to me that I worked toward was when I worked toward getting a video game box. I went to the store and saw it and thougt it was cool.

It played a snow Boarding game. I reelling liked that game so I called my dad over to see I had found a game box.

> The writer mistakenly uses *exited* instead of *excited*, possibly confusing a reader.

He was not as exited as I was. We went back home without the game box but I got it later and the Snow Boarding game. I had ketp asking my dad could we get it. Eventually he said we could after nine hundreds time of me asking. He said we could get it but I had to do some jobs first.

> The writer includes the nouns *house* and *yard*, but sensory details are lacking.

I did not like this. I cleaned up the house and cleaned up the yard, and did lots of other things, and it took a long time. I did ALL of this and then guess what??? I got the SNOW BORDING Game! This is the time I worked to a goal and got what was important to me.

Name _____ Date _____

Written Composition: Personal Narrative

LOOK

Look at the picture in the box below.

THINK

Everyday things become more special when we share them with others. Think of a special day you spent with a family member or friend. Remember what happened that day and why it was so special.

WRITE

Write a one-page personal narrative about a special day you spent with a family member or friend.

Tip

Before you begin writing, brainstorm reasons the day you chose was special.

As you write your composition, remember to —

❏ describe a day with a family member or friend.

❏ organize ideas in order and use transitions.

❏ develop your ideas with details and feelings.

❏ use correct spelling and punctuation.

❏ make sure your composition is just one page.

Tip

When you have finished your draft, reread it to make sure you have chosen the best adjectives and verbs to describe your experience.

Name _____ Date _____

Sample Response: Personal Narrative

> Write a one-page personal narrative about a special day you spent
> with a family member or friend.

The writer includes words that describe his thoughts and feelings.

The writer refers to details in the previous paragraph to show a progression of ideas.

Today was the day! My mom, brother, Grandma Lopez, and I were going to FUN ZONE! Fun zone is a huge park that has roller coasters, water slides, and a wave pool. It's pretty awesome.

Everything was going great until my brother got sick. My mom said she had to take care of him, but since we already bought tickets, I should go with my Grandma. I knew Grandma Lopez would not want to go on any of the rides. So I guess we were going to the NOT Fun zone.

When we got to the Park I was depressed. I figured we'd go look at the gift shop and maybe eat some lunch. Then I heard a voice calling my name. "Roberto!" I looked up and there was Grandma standing in line for the WILD DRAGON, the craziest roller coaster in the Park! I ran over to her and asked, "What are you doing?"

She said, "I don't know about you, Roberto, but I'm here to have fun!"

She wasn't joking! We ended up going on all of the rides I wanted + we had a blast. I'll never forget that special day I spent with my grandma at FUN Zone.

Sample Response: Personal Narrative

> **Write a one-page personal narrative about a special day you spent with a family member or friend.**

Summer is too hot! is an extra detail that does not belong in the story.

A special day I spent with a family member or friend was the I spent with my big brother. He was at colege but then he came home for the summer. Summer is TOO HOT! So we did some fun stuff.

First we played basketball outside at the hoop. Then we had some lemonade that Mom made. it was cold and sweet. After we played some video games. He beat me at this one, but I beat him at the next one. I'm the best player of my frends.

The writer just tells basic details like *We ate pizza for dinner.* More interesting words would improve the writer's descriptions of the experience.

We ate pizza for dinner. We watched a movie on tv after. Then we played a game with my mom and dad and brother. Then we went to bed.

The END

Name _____ Date _____

Written Composition: Expository

TEKS 4.15B, 4.15C, 4.15D, 4.18A(i), 4.18A(ii), 4.18A(iii)

READ

Read the sentences in the box below.

> A healthy lifestyle can help you feel physically strong and give you more energy. It also can lift your mood and keep you from getting sick. For these reasons, many people try to follow a healthy lifestyle.

THINK

Think of things a person can do to live a healthy life.

Tip
Before you begin writing, visualize what a person can do to follow a healthy lifestyle.

WRITE

Write a one-page expository composition that explains what a person can do to live a healthy life.

As you write your composition, remember to —

❏ think about a central idea—how to live a healthy life.

❏ organize your ideas in an order that makes sense, and use transitions to connect those ideas.

❏ develop your ideas using facts, details, and explanations.

❏ use correct spelling, capitalization, punctuation, grammar, and sentences.

❏ make sure your composition is no longer than one page.

Tip
Make sure your topic sentence introduces the central idea. Also make sure you have a concluding statement.

Name _____ Date _____

Sample Response: Expository

> Write a one-page expository composition that explains what a person can do to live a healthy life.

The writer establishes a central idea in the topic sentence.

A person can do many things to live a healthy life. The most important things are exercising, eating right, and sleeping.

Did you know that you can exercise by yourself or with others? Running is a great way to exercise by yourself. Football is an awesome way to exercise with other people.

Eating three meals a day is also very important. At the store, you have tons of fantastic choices. You can't go wrong with whole grains, fruits, and vegetables. Just remember that fruits and vegetables can spoil fast. So always look for expiration dates.

Sleeping is really important, too. When you sleep, your body recharges itself. Eight hours a night is just enough to make that happen. In the morning, you will wake up feeling refreshed and ready to start the day!

The writer provides a strong concluding statement.

So now you know what to do. Exercise every day, eat the right kinds of foods at every meal, and get a good night's sleep every night. That's all you need for healthy living.

Grade 4: Expository

Sample Response: Expository

> Write a one-page expository composition that explains what a person can do to live a healthy life.

Eating good foods is what is needed to live a healthy life. Good foods give you energy and help you do things.

Do you know all the good foods you can eat?

Veggies are a good food like Tomateos that grow on bushes. Tomateos make lots of different foods we eat.

Catchup is one of the foods from tomatoes. It is delishus on burgers. Did you know the bread on burgers is healthy for you? Bread is on the pearamid we eat from.

Fruits they taste reelly good. They come from trees. Apples, oranges, cherrys bananas watermelons Yum!

All of these things mean goodness for your body. You can have energy and run and play! When you run and play you are getting exersise This is important you're your helth.

The writer misspells the word *tomatoes* and includes an unnecessary detail about where tomatoes grow.

The writer mistakenly uses *you're* instead of *for*, possibly confusing a reader.

Written Composition: Expository

LOOK

Look at the picture in the box below.

THINK

Friends are people who like each other and who help each other.

Think of the qualities you look for in your own friends. Then think about what it means to be a good friend to someone.

WRITE

Write a one-page expository composition that explains how to be a good friend.

> **Tip**
> Before you begin writing, make a list of the qualities you look for in a friend.

As you write your composition, remember to —

❏ think about a central idea—being a good friend.

❏ organize ideas in order and use transitions.

❏ develop your ideas with details and feelings.

❏ use correct spelling and punctuation.

❏ make sure your composition is not more than one page.

> **Tip**
> Check to make sure all of your details tell information about the central idea.

Name _____ Date _____

Sample Response: Expository

> Write a one-page expository composition that explains how to be a good friend.

The writer develops each idea with specific details and examples that tell about the central idea.

The writer chooses thoughtful words like *loyal* and *honest*.

Basically my rule is this: Treat your friends like you would like them to treat you. If you follow this rule you will be good friends.

IF you make a promise to a friend Keep it. After all isn't that what you would want? I once told my friend I would go to her dance recital. Then my dad asked me to go to a movie the same night. I told him "no" because I had to go to Kelli's dance recital.

Once my friend was going to ride her bike on a big bike ramp, but I told her it was too big for her and too dangerous. I Knew she really wanted to do it but I was being honest. She got upset, but she was glad I was honest. I would want her to do the same thing.

Friends care about each other. If your friend is sad you should ask them why. Then you should listen to them. If you can, tell them how to fix the problem. Sometimes it's just nice to talk to someone. RIGHT?

A good friend is loyol, honest, and cares about you. And that is what you should do for all of your friends, too, if you want them to call you A GOOD FRIEND!

Grade 4: Expository

Sample Response: Expository

Write a one-page expository composition that explains how to be a good friend.

Listen up! Here is how to be a good friend. Take my advice and you will have lots of friends, Just LIKE ME!

First you have to hang out with your friend. If they say they want to go to the mall you shdd go to the mall with them. If you see your friend buying something that is not good or ugly, say "STOP IT!". Like if your friend tries on Red shoes. Second friends invite each other to parties. If you are having a party, INVITE your friend!

Friends Tell friends stuff. If you have a secret you can tell your friend. Your friend can tell a secret too. BUT don't tell anyone else the secret or else you wont be friends anymore. But that is okay if your friend told your secret because then you dont want them to be your friend really. DO YOU?

The writer includes an incomplete sentence, making it harder for the reader to understand the writer's ideas.

The writer forgets to add a concluding statement that summarizes the central idea.

Grade 4: Expository

Written Composition:
Personal Narrative

READ

Read the story in the box below.

> Jacob looked through the instruction manual for
> his sister's new bike. She had been trying to put the
> bike together all morning and finally stopped to have
> some lunch. Jacob picked up a wrench and got to
> work. An hour later when his sister came outside,
> she found a shiny new bike ready to go. Jacob smiled
> at her. He never knew he was so handy with tools.

THINK

Think of something you are good at doing. Then remember when
you first realized you were good at doing it.

WRITE

Write a one-page personal narrative about a time when you
realized you were good at doing something.

As you write your composition, remember to —

❏ describe a personal experience—a time when you realized you
   were good at something.

❏ organize your ideas in an order that makes sense and connect
   those ideas using transitions.

❏ develop your ideas with details that will help the reader
   understand your experience and your feelings.

❏ use correct spelling, capitalization, punctuation, grammar,
   and sentences.

❏ make sure your composition is just one page.

Name _____ Date _____

Written Composition:
Personal Narrative

LOOK

Look at the picture in the box below.

THINK

Sometimes things do not turn out the way we planned. Think of a time when things did not go the way you expected. Think about what you wanted to happen and what actually happened.

WRITE

Write a one-page personal narrative about a day when things did not turn out the way you planned.

As you write your composition, remember to —

❑ describe a personal experience—a day in which things did not turn out how you planned.

❑ organize your ideas in an order that makes sense and connect those ideas using transitions.

❑ develop your ideas with details that will help the reader understand your experience.

❑ use correct spelling, capitalization, punctuation, grammar, and sentences.

❑ make sure your composition is no longer than one page.

Written Composition: Expository

TEKS 4.15B, 4.15C, 4.15D, 4.18A(i), 4.18A(ii), 4.18A(iii)

READ

Read the sentences in the box below.

> A community is a place where a group of people lives and works together. It can include homes, businesses, and parks. Sometimes people see a problem in their community. They work to help fix the problem and make the community a better place. When this happens, everyone in the community can benefit.

THINK

Think of a problem in your community. Then think about what you could do to help fix the problem and make your community better.

WRITE

Write a one-page expository composition that explains how you can help make your community a better place.

As you write your composition, remember to —

❏ think about a central idea—how you can help make your community a better place.

❏ organize your ideas in an order that makes sense and use transitions to connect those ideas.

❏ develop your ideas using facts, details, and explanations.

❏ use correct spelling, capitalization, punctuation, grammar, and sentences.

❏ make sure your composition is no longer than one page.

Name _____ Date _____

Written Composition:
Expository

LOOK

Look at the picture in the box below.

THINK

Many people have an activity they enjoy doing. It might be a hobby like playing an instrument, or a sport like playing baseball.

Think of your favorite hobby or sport. Then think of why you like it and how you would introduce it to someone else.

WRITE

Write a one-page expository composition that tells why you like your favorite hobby or sport and that introduces it to others.

As you write your composition, remember to —

❏ think about a central idea—your favorite hobby or sport.

❏ organize your ideas in an order that makes sense and connect ideas using transitions.

❏ develop your ideas using facts and details.

❏ use correct spelling and punctuation.

❏ make sure your composition is just one page.

Revising

After you have finished the first draft of a composition, you still have work to do. The next step is **revising**. Revising means fixing problems in your writing such as parts that do not make sense or ideas that are out of order. Revising includes adding, deleting, and moving text.

When you revise your paper, you can delete details or sentences that you do not need, and you can add or move details or sentences to better support the main idea. You can also make sure that you have used simple and compound sentences correctly and that you have written with the audience in mind.

Read this chart to learn more about ways to revise your writing.

Check
• Include a topic sentence with a main idea, sentences that support the main idea, and a concluding statement that sums up the ideas.
• Make sure all of the examples, facts, and details that you included help the reader understand your main idea.
Add
• Add transition words, such as *before*, *for example*, and *because*.
Delete
• Delete words, sentences, and paragraphs that are not about the main idea.
• Delete facts that do not give information about the main idea, even if they are interesting.
Move
• Move a word, sentence, or paragraph if it would fit better in another part of the paper.
Sentences
• Use a variety of simple and compound sentences.
• When possible, combine related ideas into one sentence.

Name _____ Date _____

Revising

TEKS 4.15C, 4.18A(i), 4.18A(ii), 4.18A(iii)

> **Read the introduction and the passage below. Then read each question. Fill in the circle of the correct answer on your answer document.**

Julio wrote this report about a special law enforcement group. He needs help revising it. Read his report and think about the changes he should make. Then answer the questions that follow.

The Texas Rangers

(1) The Rangers have been around since the earliest European settlements in the state. (2) They have an interesting history. (3) Many books have been written about the Texas Rangers. (4) I read a book about them last year. (5) Movies have also been made about this famous group.

(6) The Rangers formed in 1823. (7) Stephen Austin was the leader of a growing colony at that time. (8) Austin posted a help-wanted ad. (9) He knew it was important to protect the land. (10) People needed to feel safe in the colony, too. (11) There wasn't any police force or other security. (12) It called for ten men to provide protection wherever it was needed.

(13) Through the years, the Rangers have acted as scouts, horsemen, and defenders. (14) Their role continues today. (15) The Rangers perform many duties.

> **Tip**
>
> If a detail does not belong, delete it.

> **Tip**
>
> Think of details that Julio could add to help the reader understand the main idea.

© Houghton Mifflin Harcourt Publishing Company

Grade 4: Revising

1 Which is the **BEST** topic sentence for this report?

   A Texas has a group called the Texas Rangers that does good things.

   B Law enforcement is a difficult job no matter where you live.

   C Law enforcement is the job of different groups.

   D The Texas Rangers are an important law-enforcement group in the state of Texas.

TEKS 4.18A(i)

2 Which sentence does **NOT** belong in this report?

   F Sentence 2

   G Sentence 4

   H Sentence 6

   J Sentence 7

TEKS 4.15C

> **Tip**
>
> Look for a sentence that does not give the reader important information about the Texas Rangers.

3 Where should sentence 8 move to make more sense in the report?

   A After sentence 6

   B After sentence 9

   C After sentence 11

   D No revision is needed.

TEKS 4.15C

> **Tip**
>
> Try moving sentence 8 after each of the sentences in the answer choices. Check to see if the paragraph makes more sense.

4 What is the **BEST** way to combine sentences 13 and 14?

   F Through the years, the Rangers have acted as scouts, horsemen, and defenders, but their role continues today.

   G Through the years, the Rangers have acted as scouts, horsemen, and defenders, their role continues today.

   H Through the years, the Rangers have acted as scouts, horsemen, and defenders, and their role continues today.

   J Through the years, the Rangers have acted as scouts, horsemen, and defenders, and their role, continues today.

TEKS 4.15C

GO ON

Name _____ Date _____

5 Which sentence could **BEST** follow sentence 15?

A For example, they investigate crimes and search for missing persons.

B They would ride horses to catch criminals who ran from the Rangers.

C A police force was later used to help keep the state of Texas safe.

D You can see good deeds the Rangers did if you watch a movie about them.

TEKS 4.18A(ii)

Tip
Look for the sentence that gives an important detail about the main idea of the paragraph.

6 Which sentence would **BEST** conclude this report?

F Law enforcement is just one way people can make a difference.

G The Texas Rangers helped the community many years ago.

H Stephen Austin found his own solution to a difficult problem.

J The people of Texas should be proud of their Texas Rangers.

TEKS 4.18A(iii)

Grade 4: Revising

Read the introduction and the passage below. Then read each question. Fill in the correct answer on your answer document.

Maria started writing this story about a class pet. Read Maria's story and look for corrections and improvements she should make. Then answer the questions that follow.

Charlie the Hedgehog

(1) Last year my class had a pet hedgehog named Charlie. (2) It was the first time I had ever seen a hedgehog. (3) Charlie was small and slept most of the day, so he made a good animal for our classroom. (4) Hedgehogs are nocturnal animals. (5) That means they are awake at night. (6) That also means they sleep during the day. (7) We put a covering over Charlie's cage so he could sleep.

(8) My friend Angelo was on vacation. (9) When school ended, my teacher asked if anyone wanted to take Charlie for the summer. (10) I asked Mom and Dad. (11) I told my parents I would treat him well.

(12) The first thing we did was get Charlie's cage ready. (13) Next, we put in his dishes for food and water. (14) Then we added an exercise wheel that he used every night. (15) We put in a little box he could hide in to get away from light or noise during the day.

(16) One afternoon my friends came over to see Charlie. (17) I put Charlie in his exercise ball, and we let him roll around the house. (18) My brother's room was so messy. (19) When I wanted to put Charlie back in his cage, we couldn't find him anywhere! (20) We looked all over.

Grade 4: Revising Practice

Name _____ Date _____

(21) Then I thought, "If I were Charlie, where would I go to get away from noise and light?" (22) I knew right away. (23) He was in the closet. (24) He was sleeping in his exercise ball!

---

1 Where should sentence 2 move to make more sense in the story?

Ⓐ Before sentence 1

B After sentence 3

C After sentence 4

D No revision is needed.

TEKS 4.15C

2 Which is the **BEST** way to combine sentences 5 and 6?

F That means they are awake at night and they sleep during the day.

Ⓖ That means they are awake at night and that also means they sleep during the day.

H That means they are awake at night they sleep during the day.

J That means they are awake at night, sleep during the day.

TEKS 4.15C

3 Which sentence does **NOT** belong in this story?

A Sentence 1

B Sentence 7

C Sentence 8

D Sentence 9

TEKS 4.15C

4 Which sentence could **BEST** follow sentence 10?

F "You can't forget to feed him and clean his cage!"

G My teacher said I could take the rest of Charlie's food home, too.

H My friend has a pet dog, so she didn't think she could take Charlie home.

J They said I could have Charlie for the summer if I promised to take care of him.

TEKS 4.15C

Grade 4: Revising Practice

5 Where should sentence 11 move to make more sense in the story?

A Before sentence 7

B Before sentence 8

C Before sentence 9

D No revision is needed.

TEKS 4.15C

6 Which transition word should be added to the beginning of sentence 15?

F Before

G Finally

H Because

J First

TEKS 4.15C

7 Which sentence does **NOT** belong in the story?

A Sentence 16

B Sentence 17

C Sentence 18

D Sentence 19

TEKS 4.15C

8 Which is the **BEST** way to combine sentences 23 and 24?

F He was in the closet, he was sleeping in his exercise ball!

G He was in the closet and he was sleeping, in his exercise ball!

H He was in the closet, and he was sleeping in his exercise ball!

J He was in the closet, or he was sleeping in his exercise ball!

TEKS 4.15C

Grade 4: Revising Practice

> **Read the introduction and the passage below. Then read each question.**
> **Fill in the correct answer on your answer document.**

Shayla wrote this report about a famous person from Texas. Read Shayla's report and think about the changes she should make. Then answer the questions that follow.

Barbara Jordan

(1) She was born on February 21, 1936. (2) She was born in Houston, Texas. (3) She earned a degree from Texas Southern University when she was only 20 years old. (4) Barbara Jordan was intelligent and a very good student. (5) This was a year earlier than most college students earn a degree. (6) Then she went to law school to become a lawyer.

(7) Barbara Jordan was very interested in government. (8) Her father was a minister. (9) In 1966, she became the first African American senator from Texas since 1883. (10) This was a big accomplishment. (11) In 1968, she won that race again. (12) In 1972, she was the Texas governor for just one day. (13) This made her the first African American woman governor in the history of the United States.

(14) Barbara Jordan cared about people. (15) She also cared deeply about her country. (16) She spoke out for equal rights. (17) She also wanted people to work together to make America great.

(18) When Barbara Jordan was 43 years old, she stopped working for the government. (19) She started teaching at the University of Texas. (20) She still spoke at special events for her country. (21) She was known for giving

GO ON

Grade 4: Revising Practice

© Houghton Mifflin Harcourt Publishing Company

Name _____ Date _____

speeches that inspired people. (22) In 1994, she received the Presidential Medal of Freedom. (23) This award showed how important Barbara Jordan was to the state of Texas and the United States. (24) Barbara Jordan received other medals and honors for her work.

1 Which is the **BEST** topic sentence for this report?

  A Barbara Jordan deserved all of the medals and honors she received.

  B Barbara Jordan would become a senator of Texas one day.

  C Barbara Jordan is an important person in United States history.

  D Barbara Jordan was born in the state of Texas.

TEKS 4.18A(i)

2 What is the **BEST** way to combine sentences 1 and 2?

  F She was born on February 21, 1936 and was born in Houston, Texas.

  G She was born on February 21, 1936, in Houston, Texas.

  H She was born in Houston, Texas and also was born on February 21, 1936.

  J She was born on February 21, 1936, but she was born in Houston, Texas.

TEKS 4.15C

3 Where should sentence 3 move to make more sense in the report?

  A After sentence 4

  B After sentence 5

  C After sentence 6

  D No revision is needed.

TEKS 4.15C

4 Which sentence does **NOT** belong in the second paragraph?

  F Sentence 8

  G Sentence 9

  H Sentence 11

  J Sentence 12

TEKS 4.15C

GO ON

Grade 4: Revising Practice

5 Which sentence could **BEST** follow sentence 16?

  A She was also elected to the U.S. House of Representatives.

  B The founders of our country believed that everyone should have rights.

  C She believed that everyone deserved to be treated the same way.

  D Other people have also fought for equal rights.

TEKS 4.15C

6 Which transition word should be added to the beginning of sentence 20?

  F However

  G First

  H After

  J Instead

TEKS 4.15C

7 Which sentence could **BEST** be added after sentence 21?

  A Barbara Jordan worked hard for her country.

  B In 1952, she graduated from high school with honors.

  C In 1992, she spoke at the Democratic National Convention.

  D Barbara Jordan enjoyed teaching college students.

TEKS 4.18A(ii)

8 Which sentence would **BEST** conclude this report?

  F Some people think she would have done more if she did not stop working for the government.

  G She should have continued to work for the government because she was very good at it.

  H Some of her awards are very important and should be displayed for everyone to see.

  J She is a great role model for people who are interested in the United States government.

TEKS 4.18A(iii)

TEKS 4.15D, 4.20A, 4.20B, 4.21B, 4.21C, 4.22A

Editing

Editing is one of the final stages in the writing process. When you edit your writing, you read it carefully to look for errors in grammar, punctuation, capitalization, and spelling. The goal of editing is to catch and correct your errors, especially those that may distract or confuse your readers.

Read this chart to learn more about ways to edit your writing.

Grammar

- Make sure that you have used all nouns, verbs, adjectives, and adverbs correctly.

- Be sure to use prepositions and prepositional phrases correctly.

- Check that reflexive pronouns, such as *myself* and *ourselves*, are correct.

- Make sure that the conjunction *either* is paired with *or*, and that *neither* is paired with *nor*.

- Check that sentences have complete subjects and complete predicates.

- Be sure that simple and compound sentences have correct subject-verb agreement.

Punctuation and Capitalization

- Check that you have used commas correctly in compound sentences.

- Be sure to capitalize proper nouns such as the names of people and places. You should also capitalize the names of historical events, books, languages, and nationalities.

Spelling

- Check that you have spelled homophones correctly (*they're/their/there, too/to/two*).

- Check that you have spelled irregular plurals correctly (*man/men, child/children*).

- Check that you have spelled base words, prefixes, and suffixes correctly (*-ion, -ment, -ly, dis-, pre-*).

- Check that you have spelled words with double consonants and silent letters correctly (*knee, wrap*).

- Use spelling patterns and rules to check your spelling.

Grade 4: Editing

Editing

TEKS 4.15D, 4.20A(ii), 4.20B, 4.21B(i), 4.21C(i), 4.22A(v)

> **Read the introduction and the passage below. Then read each question. Fill in the circle of the correct answer on your answer document.**

Anna started writing this narrative. She needs help editing it. Think about the changes she should make. Then answer the questions that follow.

Staying Up

(1) Most nights, Lauren had trouble falling asleep. (2) She didn't mind staying up but she didn't like being the last one awake. (3) The dark, creaky really scared her. (4) So every night at bedtime, Lauren would say to their parents, "Don't go to sleep before I do."

(5) One day in the summer, Aunt Blanche came to visit. (6) Aunt Blanche was a history teacher. (7) She loved to read books and talk about the Civil war. (8) Whenever Lauren asked Aunt Blanche to play a game or go swimming, Blanche would just say, "Maybe," rinkle her nose, and go back to reading her book.

(9) One Friday night, Lauren's parents said that they were going out and that Aunt Blanche would be babysitting. (10) When it was time for bed, Lauren croaked to Aunt Blanche, "Don't go to sleep before I do!"

(11) An hour later, Lauren was still awake. (12) She tiptoed over to Aunt Blanche's Room and peeked into it.

Tip
A compound sentence is made up of two shorter sentences joined by a comma and a conjunction.

Tip
Some words have spelling patterns that include silent letters.

© Houghton Mifflin Harcourt Publishing Company

Name _____ Date _____

TEKS 4.15D, 4.20A(ii), 4.20B, 4.21B(i), 4.21C(i), 4.22A(v)

(13) Aunt Blanche was reading a book, waiting for Lauren to fall asleep. (14) Lauren smiled to herself, went back to her room, and fell instantly asleep.

1 What change, if any, should be made in sentence 2?

A Change *staying* to **staing**

B Insert a comma after *up*

C Change *last* to **most last**

D Make no change

TEKS 4.21C(i)

2 What change, if any, is needed in sentence 3?

F Change *dark* to **darker**

G Insert **house** after *creaky*

H Delete *really*

J Make no change

TEKS 4.20B

Tip
A complete subject must include a noun.

3 What change, if any, is needed in sentence 4?

A Change *their* to **her**

B Delete the comma after *parents*

C Delete the quotation mark after the period

D Make no change

TEKS 4.15D

4 What change, if any, is needed in sentence 7?

F Insert a comma after *talk*

G Change *Civil* to **civil**

H Change *war* to **War**

J Make no change

TEKS 4.21B(i)

Tip
Historical events, such as the Boston Tea Party, are capitalized.

GO ON

Grade 4: Editing

5 What change should be made in sentence 8?

A Change *Aunt* to **aunt**

B Change *swimming* to **swiming**

C Delete the comma after *say*

D Change *rinkle* to **wrinkle**

TEKS 4.22A(v)

Tip
Look for a spelling pattern with a silent letter.

6 What change should be made in sentence 12?

F Change *tiptoed* to **tiptoes**

G Change *over* to **like**

H Change *Room* to **room**

J Insert a comma after *and*

TEKS 4.20A(ii)

Grade 4: Editing

Name _____ Date _____

Editing
PRACTICE

TEKS 4.20A(iv), 4.20A(vii),
4.20B, 4.21B(iii), 4.22A(i),
4.22A(ii), 4.22B

> **Read the introduction and the passage below. Then read each question.**
> **Fill in the circle of the correct answer on your answer document.**

William started writing this essay about an interesting sport. Read William's essay and look for corrections and improvements he should make. Then answer the questions that follow.

Karate

(1) Karate is a sport for people of all ages, from childs to adults. (2) In karate, you learn how to defend yourself by using only your hands and feet. (3) Many people like karate because it's good exercise, too!

(4) There are many storys about how and where karate started. (5) Some people believe that the sport started on an island near Japan hundreds of years ago. (6) A king became tired of war. (7) He would not his men use weapons. (8) Since his warriors had no weapons, they learned movemants, or forms, to use when they fought. (9) Teachers taught these forms to other people. (10) Through the years, more and more people studied the sport. (11) Today, people all over the world can learn these forms. (12) Many people, including americans, study these forms at karate schools.

(13) When people do karate, they often wear a white jacket and white pants. (14) Their teacher usual gives them a special belt to wear. (15) The color of the belt they wear shows how much they know. (16) A beginner wears a white belt. (17) The other colors are yellow, orange, green, blue, brown, and black. (18) People wear either a brown belt or a black belt at the two highest levels.

Name _____ Date _____

Editing
PRACTICE

TEKS 4.20A(iv), 4.20A(vii),
4.20B, 4.21B(iii), 4.22A(i),
4.22A(ii), 4.22B

(19) Sometimes people go to a competision to see how good they are.

(20) They can compete against other people of the same age and rank.

(21) They can see people at all levels of skill. (22) By watching, they can see how to get better.

---

1 What change, if any, should be made in sentence 1?

A Change *people* to **People**

B Change the comma to a period

C Change *childs* to **children**

D Make no change

TEKS 4.22A(ii)

2 What change should be made in sentence 4?

F Change *are* to **is**

G Change *storys* to **stories**

H Insert a comma after *how*

J Change *where* to **wear**

TEKS 4.22A(i)

3 What change, if any, should be made in sentence 7?

A Change *He* to **King**

B Insert **let** after *not*

C Change *use* to **used**

D Make no change

TEKS 4.20B

4 What change should be made in sentence 8?

F Insert a period after *weapons*

G Change *learned* to **learn**

H Change *movemants* to **movements**

J Change *fought* to **fouht**

TEKS 4.22B

113

Editing
PRACTICE

·TEKS 4.20A(iv), 4.20A(vii),
4.20B, 4.21B(iii), 4.22A(i),
4.22A(ii), 4.22B

5 What change, if any, should be made in sentence 12?

A Delete the comma after *people*

B Change *americans* to **Americans**

C Change *forms* to **form**

D Make no change

TEKS 4.21B(iii)

6 What change should be made in sentence 14?

F Change *usual* to **usually**

G Change *gives* to **gave**

H Change *to* to **too**

J Change the period to a question mark

TEKS 4.20A(iv)

7 What change, if any, should be made in sentence 18?

A Change *either* to **neither**

B Change *or* to **nor**

C Insert a comma after *belt*

D Make no change

TEKS 4.20A(vii)

8 What change, if any, should be made in sentence 19?

F Delete *Some* in **Sometimes**

G Change *competision* to **competition**

H Change *good* to **well**

J Make no change

TEKS 4.20A(iv)

114

Name _____ Date _____

Editing
PRACTICE

TEKS 4.15D, 4.20A(iii),
4.20A(v), 4.20A(vi), 4.21B(ii),
4.22A(iii), 4.22C, 4.22D

> **Read the introduction and the passage below. Then read each question.**
> **Fill in the circle of the correct answer on your answer document.**

Lin started writing this story about a piano recital. Read Lin's story and look for corrections and improvements she should make. Then answer the questions that follow.

The Piano Recital

(1) Last week I had my piano recital. (2) They say "practice makes perfect." (3) That may not be exactly true, but it is important! (4) Preparing for a piano recital takes a long time and a lot of work.

(5) I started with choosing the music to play. (6) I looked at all the pages in a piano book called <u>Classic Piano Songs For Everyone</u>. (7) With my teacher's help, I chose "Für Elise," a beautiful piece by Beethoven. (8) I felt that I could learn this music in time.

(9) The recital was three months away. (10) The most important thing to do was to practice. (11) Each day I practiced for a longest period of time than I had the day before. (12) After two months I could play it perfectly, but I still had to read the sheet music. (13) Finally in the last month, I could play without looking. (14) Then I knew I was ready! (15) I could hardly weight to get on the stage and play.

(16) I had to do prepare in other ways, too. (17) I had to learn to sit up straight on the piano bench. (18) Sitting up straight would make me look and feel sure of myself. (19) My teacher helped me learn to bend my fingers. (20) They should'nt be stiff. (21) I also chose my best clothes to wear.

Name _____ Date _____

Editing
PRACTICE

TEKS 4.15D, 4.20A(iii),
4.20A(v), 4.20A(vi), 4.21B(ii),
4.22A(iii), 4.22C, 4.22D

(22) On the day of the recital I sat in the front row. (23) When it was my turn, I sat down at the piano. (24) I thought only about the music. (25) My hands seemed to play by themself. (26) Then it was over and I stood up and bowed. (27) I noticed the audience for the first time. (28) The best part was the aplause! (29) My hard work had paid off.

---

1 What change is needed in sentence 6?

  A Change *looked* to **look**

  B Change *Classic* to **Clasic**

  C Change *For* to **for**

  D Add quotation marks around the book title

TEKS 4.21B(ii)

2 What change, if any, is needed in sentence 7?

  F Change *teacher's* to **teachers**

  G Change *chose* to **choose**

  H Change *piece* to **peice**

  J Make no change

TEKS 4.22D

3 What change is needed in sentence 11?

  A Change *practiced* to **practicing**

  B Change *longest* to **longer**

  C Insert a comma after *time*

  D Change *before* to **after**

TEKS 4.20A(iii)

4 What change, if any, should be made in sentence 15?

  F Change *weight* to **wait**

  G Change *on* to **in**

  H Insert a comma after *stage*

  J Make no change

TEKS 4.22C

Grade 4: Editing Practice

5 What change, if any, is needed in sentence 20?

A Change *They* to **Their**

B Change *should'nt* to **shouldn't**

C Change *stiff* to **stiffen**

D Make no change

TEKS 4.15D

6 What change should be made in sentence 22?

F Insert a comma after *recital*

G Change *I* to **myself**

H Change *sat* to **sit**

J Change *front* to **Front**

TEKS 4.20A(v)

7 What change is needed in sentence 25?

A Change *seemed* to **seamed**

B Insert a comma after *play*

C Change *themself* to **themselves**

D Change the period to a question mark

TEKS 4.20A(vi)

8 What change, if any, should be made in sentence 28?

F Insert **most** before *best*

G Change *aplause* to **applause**

H Change the exclamation mark to a period

J Make no change

TEKS 4.22A(iii)

Texas Write Source
Assessments

Name _____ Date _____

Pretest

Part 1: Basic Elements of Writing

> **Questions 1–10:** Read each sentence. Choose the best way to write the underlined part of the sentence. Fill in the circle of the correct answer on your answer document.

1 Sometimes we go <u>with</u> Grandma and Grandpa's house for the holidays.

   A for

   B to

   C of

   D Make no change

2 They keep a bedroom ready for my sister and <u>me</u>.

   F I

   G we

   H myself

   J Make no change

3 Last year we <u>gone</u> to their house in August.

   A go

   B went

   C going

   D Make no change

4 They <u>lives</u> near a big river.

   F live

   G living

   H is living

   J Make no change

5 On August 12, I caught the <u>most big</u> catfish I have ever seen.

   A bigger

   B biggest

   C most biggest

   D Make no change

6 A large bass <u>splash</u> in the river.

   F splashing

   G are splashing

   H splashes

   J Make no change

Name _____   Date _____

7 Sometimes Grandpa rows the boat
<u>heself</u>.

   A himself

   B him

   C itself

   D Make no change

8 Next Sunday Grandma <u>will play</u>
the organ for a wedding.

   F played

   G play

   H was playing

   J Make no change

9 She plays the organ <u>very good</u>
and sings beautifully.

   A very goodly

   B very gooder

   C very well

   D Make no change

10 I don't know how she can play <u>but</u> sing
at the same time.

   F or

   G and

   H yet

   J Make no change

**Questions 11–14: Read each question and fill in the circle of the correct answer
on your answer document.**

---

11 Which sentence uses a time-order
transition word?

   A Seeds can travel by floating
in the wind.

   B Beautiful white seeds fly
around and around.

   C Some seeds stick to animals
and clothing.

   D Remove seeds from your coat
before you go inside.

12 Which is an imperative sentence
that should end with a period?

   F Do we have to stay on the path

   G That tree is covered with flowers

   H Look for seeds sticking to your socks

   J Wow, look at that black and orange
bird

13 Which is a run-on sentence and should be written as two sentences?

   A Seeds float on water they ride on animals.

   B Ants plant seeds by carrying them into their holes.

   C Mud sticks to animals' feet and comes off later.

   D Violet seeds burst out of a seed pod and zoom off.

14 Which is the best way to combine these sentences?

> Seeds grow in flowers.
>
> The seeds drop to the ground.

   F Seeds grow in flowers, they drop to the ground.

   G Seeds grow in flowers, then drop to the ground.

   H Seeds grow in flowers and seeds drop to the ground.

   J Seeds grow but drop to the ground in flowers.

Questions 15–16: A student wrote this paragraph about school clothes. It may need some changes or corrections. Read the paragraph. Then read each question. Fill in the circle of the correct answer on your answer document.

School Clothes

   (1) Last year I attended a school where everyone wore the same thing. (2) I didn't like our uniforms. (3) The colors were boring, and the style was old-fashioned. (4) I had to get up very early, too. (5) My mom complained that the uniforms cost a lot. (6) This year I started at a school that doesn't have uniforms. (7) I was excited because I could wear my own clothes. (8) Every day I put on something different. (9) I like being able to wear what I want to wear to school.

15 What type of paragraph is this?

   A personal narrative

   B expository

   C book report

   D persuasive

16 Which sentence should be removed to improve this paragraph?

   F sentence 1

   G sentence 2

   H sentence 3

   J sentence 4

GO ON

Part 2: Proofreading and Editing

> **Questions 17–24: Read the passages. Choose the best way to write each underlined part. Fill in the circle of the correct answer on your answer document.**

My uncle lives in Japan. He speaks Japanese and <u>other asian</u>
                                                        17

<u>languages,</u> including Chinese. He visited my family last summer. He told

us why he likes living in Japan. He likes learning about another country

and eating <u>differnt</u> <u>kinds of Japanese food.</u> He also likes meeting people
            18   **19**

from all over the world. I want to learn other languages when I am older.

I will study <u>spanish and french</u> so I can live in another country.
              20

17 A Other asian Languages,

   B other Asian Languages,

   C other Asian languages,

   D Make no change

18 F diferent

   G different

   H difernt

   J Make no change

19 A Kinds of Japanese Food.

   B kinds of japanese food.

   C kinds of Japanese Food.

   D Make no change

20 F spanish and French

   G Spanish and French

   H Spanish and french

   J Make no change

Old Faithful Lodge
Yellowstone National Park, WY 82190
August 14, 2012

Dear Tisa,

<u>Me and my family</u> are camping in Yellowstone National Park for
    21

the whole week. It's so beautiful! Yesterday we got up early and hiked

to Fairy Falls. When we got <u>there</u> we swam around under the waterfall.
            22

At night my dad read us an essay, <u>"explorers in yellowstone."</u> We visited
                   23

some of the places we read about. I hope we see some eagles and <u>moose</u>.
                                    24

We lock up our food at night so the bears can't get it. I'll see you soon.

Your cousin,

Lily

21 A Myself and my family

   B I and my family

   C My family and I

   D Make no change

23 A "explorers in Yellowstone."

   B "Explorers in Yellowstone."

   C "Explorers in yellowstone."

   D Make no change

22 F there.

   G there,

   H there—

   J Make no change

24 F mooses

   G moss

   H moosse

   J Make no change

GO ON

Part 3: Writing

Narrative

LOOK

Look at the picture in the box below.

THINK

Think back to a day when you visited a special place. It might have been a place outdoors, such as a beach or park. It might have been a place indoors, such a museum or friend's house.

Think about why the place was special to you. Then think about the things you did that day.

WRITE

Write a narrative composition telling about a visit to a special place.

As you write your composition, remember to —

❏ focus on one experience—your visit to a special place

❏ organize your ideas in an order that makes sense, and connect the ideas with transitions

❏ develop your ideas with specific details

❏ make sure your composition is no longer than one page

Name _____ Date _____

Progress Test 1

Part 1: Basic Elements of Writing

> **Questions 1–10:** Read each sentence. Choose the best way to write the underlined part of the sentence. Fill in the circle of the correct answer on your answer document.

1 Taylor and Esteban <u>is</u> my two best friends.

   A are

   B was

   C be

   D Make no change

2 Esteban is really good <u>for</u> every sport he plays.

   F with

   G at

   H to

   J Make no change

3 He is the <u>best</u> baseball player on our Rookie League team.

   A good

   B goodest

   C more better

   D Make no change

4 He <u>has took</u> tennis lessons for three years.

   F has taken

   G has taked

   H taking

   J Make no change

5 Taylor always makes <u>myself</u> feel better when I'm upset about something.

   A I

   B me

   C we

   D Make no change

6 In an emergency, he thinks <u>fast</u> than other kids and knows just what to do.

   F faster

   G fastest

   H more fast

   J Make no change

7 All three of <u>us</u> play on the same team.

A we

B ourselves

C they

D Make no change

8 One day Taylor, Esteban, and I <u>is</u> playing softball near Taylor's house.

F was

G am

H were

J Make no change

9 While we were playing, a bee <u>stinged</u> me.

A stung

B sting

C stang

D Make no change

10 Taylor put ice on my sting, <u>but</u> it soon stopped hurting.

F if

G and

H or

J Make no change

Questions 11–14: Read each question and fill in the circle of the correct answer on your answer document.

---

11 Which is the best way to combine these two sentences?

> Louis Leakey was born in Kenya.
>
> He was born on August 7, 1903.

A Louis Leakey was born in Kenya and was born on August 7, 1903.

B Louis Leakey was born in Kenya, but on August 7, 1903.

C Louis Leakey was born in Kenya, and he was born on August 7, 1903.

D Louis Leakey was born in Kenya on August 7, 1903.

12 Which is a declarative sentence that should end with a period?

F Where did Dr. Leakey dig up the fossils

G How old these fossils must be

H He found fossils of ape-like animals that lived 14 million years ago

J When did he discover fossils of early humans

GO ON

13 Which sentence has a complete subject and a complete predicate?

A He made some amazing fossil discoveries in Africa.

B Found the remains of the earliest human being.

C One place in Africa known as the Great Rift Valley.

D Discovered tools that the early humans used.

14 Which is a run-on sentence that should be written as two sentences?

F I want to go on a trip to look for fossils.

G When our car broke down in the desert, I looked for fossils by the road.

H I found an arrowhead, some arrowheads are really old.

J It would be great to make some exciting discoveries.

Questions 15–16: A student wrote this paragraph about rocks. It may need some changes or corrections. Read the paragraph. Then read each question. Fill in the circle of the correct answer on your answer document.

Rocks Formed by Fire

(1) Fire rocks—or igneous rocks—are formed when lava cools down. (2) Some kinds of rocks are produced by volcanoes. (3) Obsidian, pumice, and granite are all fire rocks. (4) Fire rocks can be shiny, smooth, and hard, like obsidian. (5) They can also be light and full of holes, like pumice. (6) Obsidian looks like black glass and has sharp edges. (7) It forms when lava cools quickly above ground. (8) Granite forms when lava cools underground.

15 What type of paragraph is this?

A expository

B narrative

C persuasive

D book review

16 Which two sentences should be switched to improve the paragraph?

F sentences 1 and 2

G sentences 3 and 4

H sentences 5 and 6

J sentences 7 and 8

Part 2: Proofreading and Editing

> **Questions 17–24:** Read the passages. Choose the best way to write each underlined part. Fill in the circle of the correct answer on your answer document.

Last Saturday my uncle asked me to saw a dead branch off the big

beech tree in his yard. He <u>said You</u> are the only one <u>which</u> can climb up
                17   **18**

there." I climbed up and started to saw the <u>branch but</u> then we heard
                                  19

peeping sounds. On the dead branch was a nest full of hungry baby birds.

Their mouths were wide open. I fed the birds some <u>caterpillars?</u> Then I
                                            20

carefully moved the nest to another branch so the parents could find it.

17 A said "You

    B said, "you

    C said, "You

    D Make no change

18 F whom

    G who

    H what

    J Make no change

19 A branch, but

    B branch; but

    C branch: but

    D Make no change

20 F caterpillars!

    G caterpillars:

    H caterpillars.

    J Make no change

GO ON

Name _____ Date _____

600 Elm Street
Plano, Texas 75023
April 6, 2012

Mrs. Martha Roscoe
Washington Community Center
916 5th Street
Plano, TX 75023

Dear <u>Mrs. Roscoe</u>
      21

I would like to try out for the community chorus. I <u>herd</u> that you are
                    22

looking for young singers for your summer <u>concert</u>. I sing soprano. My
                        23

friends think I'm good. Could I try out sometime soon? I'm almost 10

years old. My mom says <u>its</u> okay for me to sing in your group.
           24

Sincerely,

Emily Wu

21 A Mrs. Roscoe:

   B Mrs. Roscoe—

   C Mrs. Roscoe;

   D Make no change

23 A consurt

   B concurt

   C consert

   D Make no change

22 F herded

   G heard

   H heared

   J Make no change

24 F it's

   G its'

   H its's

   J Make no change

GO ON

Name _____ Date _____

Part 3: Writing   Expository

READ

Everyone is good at something. When we want to learn how to do something, we go to someone who's good at it.

THINK

Think of something you are good at. It might be something you know how to make, such as a sand castle. It might be something you know how to do, such as choosing a fun video game.

WRITE

Write an expository composition naming what you are good at and explaining how to do it.

As you write your composition, remember to —

❏ focus on one thing and the steps for how to do it

❏ arrange your steps in an order that makes sense, and connect the steps with transitions

❏ include details that help you explain the steps

❏ make sure your composition is no longer than one page

Name _____ Date _____

Progress Test 2
Part 1: Basic Elements of Writing

> **Questions 1–10:** Read each sentence. Choose the best way to write the underlined part of the sentence. Fill in the circle of the correct answer on your answer document.

1 Earthworms may be the <u>importantest</u> creatures on Earth.

  A more important

  B importanter

  C most important

  D Make no change

2 <u>In</u> one cubic foot of soil, there may be two dozen earthworms.

  F At

  G Among

  H Through

  J Make no change

3 An <u>earthworms'</u> diet includes mostly soil and leaves.

  A earthworm's

  B earthworm

  C earthworms

  D Make no change

4 Some worms pull leaves down into <u>its</u> holes to eat.

  F his

  G their

  H theirs

  J Make no change

5 Last night we <u>finded</u> dozens of night crawlers on the lawn.

  A find

  B finding

  C found

  D Make no change

6 Some earthworms <u>eats</u> half their weight in food every day.

  F eating

  G eat

  H eaten

  J Make no change

GO ON

7 Many garden supply stores <u>sells</u> worms to gardeners.

  A are sold

  B selling

  C sell

  D Make no change

8 Worms enrich the soil <u>naturally</u>.

  F more natural

  G naturaller

  H naturallest

  J Make no change

9 Is that a snake, <u>and</u> is it a giant worm?

  A or

  B nor

  C but

  D Make no change

10 Tom's pet snake has <u>growed</u> 12 inches in the past year.

  F grew

  G grown

  H growing

  J Make no change

Questions 11–14: Read each question and fill in the circle of the correct answer on your answer document.

---

11 Which is an interrogative sentence that should end with a question mark?

  A Where did you get those pink feathers

  B What a weird mask

  C I can make the perfect costume with that cloth

  D Wait until I've finished sewing the cape

12 Which has a complete subject and a complete predicate?

  F Saw a scary movie last night.

  G The handsome man and the beautiful lady.

  H Stallions ran up the mountain road to the castle.

  J Thunder and lightning on top of the castle.

Name _____ Date _____

13 Which is a run-on sentence that should be written as two sentences?

    A I made a green bug costume with purple horns.

    B Sadie wore the clown costume, she changed into a princess.

    C Dressed in shiny black and blue, Marshall looked like a giant beetle.

    D No one knew it was Ping inside the leopard suit.

14 Which is the best way to combine these sentences?

> Irene made costumes for the play.
>
> Irene is a talented clothing designer.

    F Irene made costumes and Irene is a talented clothing designer.

    G Irene made costumes for the play, then she is a talented clothing designer.

    H Irene made costumes for the play, later she was a talented clothing designer.

    J Irene made costumes for the play because she is a talented clothing designer.

Questions 15–16: A student wrote this paragraph about making dinner. It may need some changes or corrections. Read the paragraph. Then read each question. Fill in the circle of the correct answer on your answer document.

Spaghetti Night

(1) Wednesday is our family's spaghetti night. (2) It's the night my sister Jess, my brother Ezra, and I make dinner. (3) She makes sure no one gets hurt. (4) Spaghetti is fairly easy to make. (5) We boil water, cook the spaghetti, and heat up sauce. (6) Sometimes all three of us make the salad together, but that's mostly my job. (7) Ezra usually makes dessert.

15 What type of paragraph is this?

    A response to a text

    B expository

    C personal narrative

    D persuasive

16 Where should this sentence be added to make the paragraph better?

> Jess is 15 and has been cooking for a while.

    F between sentences 1 and 2

    G between sentences 2 and 3

    H between sentences 3 and 4

    J between sentences 5 and 6

GO ON

Part 2: Proofreading and Editing

> **Questions 17–24: Read the passages. Choose the best way to write each underlined part. Fill in the circle of the correct answer on your answer document.**

A New Country

In 1776 Great Britain's colonies in America wanted their freedom.

Their representatives met and <u>made</u> a document, the <u>Declaration of</u>
                                         17   **18**

<u>Independence</u>. This document declared that the people in the colonies

wanted three important <u>things; life,</u> liberty, and the pursuit of happiness.
                                         19

George Washington read the document to his troops during the

<u>revolutionary war</u>. His soldiers were stirred by the powerful words. They
    20

fought through a long, freezing winter and eventually won their country's

freedom.

17 A maid

   B maide

   C maked

   D Make no change

19 A things: life,

   B things, life,

   C things. life,

   D Make no change

18 F declaration of independence

   G Declaration of independence

   H Declaration Of Independence

   J Make no change

20 F revolutionary War

   G Revolutionary war

   H Revolutionary War

   J Make no change

Name _____ Date _____

8801 Fairfield Avenue
Taylor, TX 76574
September 18, 2012

Ms. Delia Klein
Visitor Information Center
McDonald Observatory
Fort Davis, TX 79734

Dear Ms. Klein:

Our class plans to visit the McDonald Observatory. We would really like

to watch the night sky through the telescope. We <u>learns</u> about the moon
                                                   21

and the other <u>planet's</u> in our solar system. We would like to see the moon
              22

up close, and the next full moon will be on October 29. Would that be a

good time for us to <u>come?</u> Please call Ms. Chaney at Hamilton School in
                    23

<u>Taylor, texas</u>, to set up a time.
   24
Sincerely,

Joy Diallo

21 A has learned

   B are learning

   C learning

   D Make no change

23 A come!

   B come.

   C come;

   D Make no change

22 F planets

   G planets'

   H planets's

   J Make no change

24 F taylor, texas

   G taylor, Texas

   H Taylor, Texas

   J Make no change

Name _____ Date _____

Part 3: Writing   Expository

READ

You probably know how to play several games. How did you learn to play them?
One easy way is having someone teach you.

THINK

Think of a simple game you like to play. For example, it might be a card game or
a board game. It might be an alphabet game, or it might be a guessing game
such as "I Spy."

WRITE

Write an expository composition naming the game and explaining how to play it.

As you write your composition, remember to —

❏ focus on one game and explain how to play it

❏ organize the ideas in an order that makes sense, and connect the ideas
with transitions

❏ include details that help explain how to play the game

❏ make sure your composition is no longer than one page

Post-test

Part 1: Basic Elements of Writing

> **Questions 1–10:** Read each sentence. Choose the best way to write the underlined part of the sentence. Fill in the circle of the correct answer on your answer document.

1 Last week, Alex and Madison <u>drawed</u> a comic book with pen and ink.

   A drew

   B drewed

   C drawn

   D Make no change

2 Today, either Alex <u>or</u> Madison will color in the drawings.

   F nor

   G but

   H and

   J Make no change

3 Madison usually <u>write</u> the words herself.

   A writed

   B written

   C writes

   D Make no change

4 Tonya is making a statue of a dragon <u>from</u> clay.

   F by

   G for

   H under

   J Make no change

5 Tonya <u>has became</u> very interested in dragons lately.

   A becomes

   B was becoming

   C has become

   D Make no change

6 While <u>her</u> was at the library, Tonya saw a book on dragons.

   F it

   G she

   H they

   J Make no change

Name _____ Date _____

7 <u>Tonya's</u> clay dragon is orange with blue fire coming out of the mouth.

   A Tonyas

   B Tonyas'

   C Tonyas's

   D Make no change

8 She formed the dragon shape <u>very quick</u>.

   F very quickly

   G very quicker

   H real quick

   J Make no change

9 Making the wings was <u>hardest</u> than making the body.

   A hardiest

   B harder

   C hardly

   D Make no change

10 One of the wings <u>are</u> longer than the other.

   F is

   G were

   H be

   J Make no change

Questions 11–14: Read each question and fill in the circle of the correct answer on your answer document.

---

11 Which uses a transition word that shows a conclusion?

   A I was the last one to finish the math problem.

   B I have always liked working with numbers.

   C I finally understood how to multiply fractions.

   D Learning math really makes me use brain power.

12 Which is the best way to combine these sentences?

> Darrell likes to go fishing.
>
> He also likes to go swimming.

   F Darrell likes to go fishing and likes to go swimming, too.

   G Darrell likes to go fishing, and he likes to go swimming.

   H Darrell likes to go fishing and swimming.

   J Darrell and he like to go fishing and swimming.

Name _____ Date _____

13 Which is a declarative sentence that should end with a period?

    A Look out for that speeding boat

    B I'll just watch the fish in the river

    C How many boats did you count

    D Go get your fishing pole

14 Which is a run-on sentence that should be written as two sentences?

    F My mother was born on a houseboat, she lived there for two years.

    G When we need something, we can walk to a store in town.

    H We can catch fish, clean them, and cook them all in one place.

    J A duck just dove into the water looking for fish.

Questions 15–16: A student wrote this paragraph about getting a pet. It may need some changes or corrections. Read the paragraph. Then read each question. Fill in the circle of the correct answer on your answer document.

A Pet Snake

(1) I think my parents should let me get a pet snake. (2) Snakes can make good pets because they are easy to care for and fascinating to watch. (3) Snakes need relatively little special care or attention. (4) They are basically nocturnal, which means they sleep most of the day. (5) Many snakes eat mice and other small rodents. (6) However, they don't need darkness in order to sleep, so you don't need to keep a room dark all day. (7) Some snakes will eat frozen, pre-killed mice, but others prefer to catch their own mice live. (8) The house won't have a mouse problem any more!

15 What type of paragraph is this?

    A personal narrative

    B persuasive

    C expository

    D response to a text

16 Which two sentences should be switched to organize the paragraph better?

    F sentences 1 and 2

    G sentences 4 and 5

    H sentences 5 and 6

    J sentences 7 and 8

Part 2: Proofreading and Editing

> **Questions 17–24:** Read the passages. Choose the best way to write each underlined part. Fill in the circle of the correct answer on your answer document.

Islands in the Caribbean area have many wonderful kinds of music.

Salsa and reggae are two popular styles. Some kinds of music in this area

arrived with people who came from <u>Africa, Europe, and the Americas</u>.
                                                                    17

Each <u>groups</u> unique music mixed with the beat of native islanders'
         18

drums. People use <u>medal</u> cans to make a special kind of drum, called a
                          19

steel <u>drum!</u> It is played all over the Caribbean, especially for dancing.
          20

17 A Africa Europe and the Americas

   B Africa Europe, and the Americas

   C Africa, Europe, and, the Americas

   D Make no change

19 A mettle

   B metal

   C meddle

   D Make no change

18 F group's

   G groups'

   H groups's

   J Make no change

20 F drum;

   G drum?

   H drum.

   J Make no change

GO ON

Name _____ Date _____

108 Sycamore Street
Big Spring, TX 79739
March 25, 2012

Dear Aunt Helen,

Thanks for the great present! It arrived on <u>friday, March 23</u>. I was
21

very pleased to get the book *<u>the celery stalks at midnight</u>* for my birthday.
22

Because I liked it so much, I was inspired to write a story about myself

titled <u>"How I Solve Mysteries at Bedtime."</u> When my friend Jorge read
23

my new book, he said, <u>What a great book!</u> I totally agree.
24

Love,

Eddie

21 A friday, march 23

 B Friday, march 23

 C Friday, March 23

 D Make no change

23 A "How I Solve Mysteries At Bedtime."

 B "How I solve mysteries at bedtime."

 C "How I solve Mysteries at Bedtime."

 D Make no change

22 F *The Celery Stalks at Midnight*

 G *The celery stalks at midnight*

 H *The celery stalks at Midnight*

 J Make no change

24 F "What a great book"!

 G "What a great book!"

 H "What a great book!

 J Make no change

GO ON

Part 3: Writing   Narrative

READ

Doing things by yourself can be fun. But some things are better when shared with others. Many things are more fun if you can do them with a friend.

THINK

Think of a time when you did something really special with a friend. For example, it might have been a trip somewhere or a sleepover at your friend's house.

Think about what made the experience special. Then think about the events that made up the experience.

WRITE

Write a narrative composition telling about a special time you shared with a friend.

As you write your composition, remember to —

❏ focus on one experience—a special time with a friend

❏ organize your ideas in an order that makes sense, and connect the ideas with transitions

❏ develop your ideas with specific details

❏ make sure your composition is no longer than one page